GOES WELL WITH GRITS:

The Southern B&B Breakfast Experience

Ellen Maxwell Cowan

Goes Well with Grits: The Southern B&B Breakfast Experience

https://www.fireflymadison.com/

Copyright © 2021 by Ellen Maxwell Cowan

All rights reserved. No part of this publication may be reproduced in any form, or by any means, electronic or mechanical, including photocopying, recording, or any information browsing, storage, or retrieval system, without permission in writing from the publisher.

Although this publication is designed to provide accurate information in regard to the subject matter covered, the publisher and the author assume no responsibility for errors, inaccuracies, omissions, or any other inconsistencies herein. This publication is meant as a source of valuable information for the reader. However, it is not meant as a replacement for direct expert assistance. If such a level of assistance is required, the services of a competent professional should be sought.

Copyright © 2021 Ellen Maxwell Cowan

All rights reserved.

ISBN: 9798548645098

TABLE OF CONTENTS

1 – Once Upon a Time or The Story of Our B&B 1
2 – The B&B Guest or Why Am I Here? 6
3 – Making Breakfast and Memories 9
4 – Orchestrating an Atmosphere: Scents, Sights, Sounds 11
5 – Wake Up and Smell the Coffee 33
6 – Breakfast Unchained 36
7 – Ten Simple Facts About Pancakes 45
8 – House Waffles Versus the Waffle House 57
9 – The Strange Origins of Cereal for Breakfast 70
10 – Eggs or Weezy the Wonder Chicken 82
11 – The Art of Nonindustrial Bacon (and Sausage) 101
12 – The Only Right Way to Cook, Serve, and Eat Grits 111
13 – How to Make Toast Interestingly 130
14 – House Rules or Always Knock First 143
Bonus Materials 150
About the Author 151
Books by Ellie Cowan 152

1 – Once Upon a Time or The Story of Our B&B

Once upon a time, a long time ago, a little house was built. It was not as grand as some of the big places in the area, but it was solid. It overlooked the main road into town as if to say, "Welcome to Madison," and all the local people knew it.

A few years went by, and a new, big road was built in the vicinity. The road by the house became a little quieter. The house's builder, an engineer, moved away. A new family moved in and made some additions to the structure. Then, there were more families, and, after a time, the little house began to show its age. After an even longer time, it sat empty and seemed a bit sad.

It so happened that one day a beautiful girl appeared. She was an explorer and was passing through town. When she saw the house, it spoke to her.

"I've been waiting for you," the house said.

"I know," said the girl. "How do you feel about guests?"

"I like them fine," said the house. "But you'd better run it by the County Zoning Board."

Not long after that, the girl moved in with her helpers. There was a black chicken named Weezy, who was brave and smart. There was Posh, a big friendly white dog. The girl also brought her son, Nathaniel, who was kind and helpful but a bit of a trickster.

They named their house "The Firefly" after the little bugs that live at the edge of the woods and, in the summer, shine their light out into the world.

Before too long, the house was under construction, which, as everybody knows, involves heroes, and villains, and monsters. As in any great story, there was an abyss when everything seemed to be going wrong.

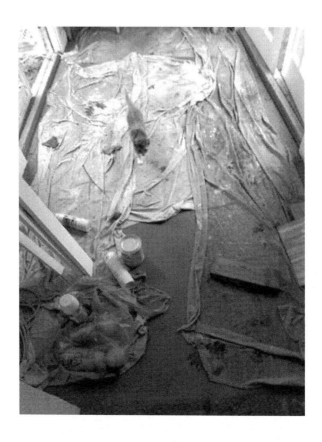

But then, one cool spring day, the disasters ended. A lady appeared—a quiet lady with a quiet little dog. She was a healer and liked to go out to sit by the pond and watch the fish. The girl and the chicken worked together to give the lady a little breakfast. She loved the place and told her friends about it. Even though the construction wasn't quite finished, the spirit of the place was emerging.

Pretty soon, more healers came from all over the world because they liked the place and the breakfast. Before long, there were other kinds of guests. There were action heroes, and beautiful brides, and a hurdy-gurdy player, and lots of regular people from everywhere. They were all on a journey of one kind or another. Some needed breakfast, and some didn't. By then, Weezy had a team of helpers, so there was plenty of breakfast to go around. The menu expanded, and there were even more options for what to serve.

No one knows exactly when it happened, but a transformation had taken place. At some point, the little house had become a beautiful destination. It was so scenic that some artists came one day and painted its picture.

The girl was transformed too. She became the Earth Goddess, the fellow traveler who welcomed all the guests and saw to their needs. If they wanted, she even made them a nice breakfast. She was the one who had endured the mud and put up with villains. Today, she walks around the grounds feeling lucky to be in a place so beautiful.

Is this the end of the story? Oh, no. The Earth Goddess occasionally goes on treasure hunts and quests and returns with something tasty or fun. The guests are on their own journey, and, to them, the little house is part of their adventure. We write all of these things down when it suits us. Every rock, tree, broken window, and piece of furniture has a story. There is always some tiny detail to fix or improve about the house as well.

Every guest changes the place a little as they become part of the story. The place changes the guests too. And everyone in town that goes by the little house still loves to look at it to see what's changed from week to week. The next chapter of The Firefly's story is still being written, but everyone there is living happily ever after, just the same.

2 – The B&B Guest or Why Am I Here?

People have all sorts of options when it comes to lodging. If someone is looking for the basics, they want standard accommodations. Standard implies something that doesn't vary from one room to the next or even from one hotel to the next if the lodging is part of a chain. Travelers who stay at chain hotels aren't interested in finding adventure. They just want a place to crash and maybe a standard breakfast the following morning that doesn't offer any surprises.

B&B travelers are a different breed altogether. They aren't focused on the destination as much as the journey. Anything that promises a unique experience will get their attention. This starts with the B&B structure itself, which is one of a kind and not usually found in tract housing developments. The rooms inside are equally unique, and each one is decorated using a different theme. Many B&Bs offer private bathrooms and separate entrances for guests.

The features described above pretty much fit The Firefly, which is actually somebody's home. The property has a few chickens, a pretty art studio, and is surrounded by nature. The three guest house rooms have separate entrances and some comforting amenities, while the three rooms in the main house are pleasantly decorated with period furniture. The entire goal of every B&B is to offer an exceptional experience to every guest. Not standard, exceptional.

3 – Making Breakfast and Memories

Because we're producing a product, and that product is an exceptional guest experience, a big component of the experience is breakfast. In fact, it is our single best way of enhancing a guest's stay. After all, "Breakfast" is half of the name of every B&B.

When we first started out, we needed to learn a lot about breakfast in general and how to serve breakfast to a happy crowd of guests in particular. There are plenty of similarities between serving breakfast to a group of guests and serving a meal to a big family. More on that later. Suffice it to say that a big family is probably more complicated.

The first part of your journey as a traveler is to think about breakfast as an event in your day. Breakfast is one of the main motivations for staying at a B&B and one of the biggest features that makes the stay memorable. It makes sense to think about breakfast as both a meal and a social event.

4 – Orchestrating an Atmosphere: Scents, Sights, Sounds

Our first task as B&B proprietors was to set up a breakfast room that could allow guests to mingle if they were so inclined. Breakfast is a time for information exchange, especially when conference groups are having a preliminary chat before their local meeting that day. We've come to find out there is a science behind the breakfast room set-up.

Engaging the Senses

The process of deliberately engaging the senses in the dining experience is called neurogastronomy. This includes the sensations you experience before and after your meal. So, in setting up a breakfast room, we needed to figure out how to appeal to each of the senses.

Aromas

The sense of smell is the easiest to engage. The coffee of choice at our place is French press, and the aroma of it fills the air early in the morning. To this, we can add the aroma of what is being served for breakfast. If you're here by yourself, the meal will probably be simple. If there are several guests staying at the same time, the scents may be more complex. We will talk about the breakfast menu in more detail as we go along.

Typically, at The Firefly, there will be the smell of eggs (because of our abundance of chickens) and bacon (local preference). According to scientific research, 80% of people like the smell of bacon, even though this is a high-overhead activity since someone needs to stand by the stove and fry it. The additional effort is worth it because the combination of coffee and bacon is usually enough to attract hungry guests to the breakfast room.

Depending on the time of year, there may also be a pleasant fireplace aroma in the house. The winter nights tend not to be long in Georgia, but sometimes the days are a bit gloomy. Since we have an abundance of firewood, we usually keep a fire going to create a cozy atmosphere.

Sounds

What follows is a true story. When we bought the place, we noticed that there were whole-house speakers. Theoretically, we should be able to broadcast anything we want. The only problem, if you want to call it that, is that we can't figure out where to plug the speakers in. The wires run through the ceiling, and despite several careful searches, we can't figure out where they end up. So, for now, we rely on other sources to provide for your listening pleasure.

Cable News

It is not at all uncommon to use TV as background noise for breakfast. This is very typical at the Hampton Inn up the road. We have come to find out that the people who do the programming for morning TV engineer their shows to attract listeners. Depending on the city, you may find yourself listening to the previous night's murder stories, how many traffic accidents you can expect on the way to your venue, and the latest panic. In some cases, you will get the Weather Channel, which is not really any better because of tornado warnings, blizzard threats, and the like.

In setting up our breakfast room, we have made a conscious effort to keep this kind of irritating jibber-jabber to a minimum. We want you to have less stress in the morning, not more. So, for the most part, you will not get blaring cable news along with your breakfast. In fact, we try to create a media detox/retreat atmosphere where we deliberately shut off social media and cable news. There is some underlying science to suggest that you should avoid information overload. Those sound bites are killing you. At The Firefly, you may, instead, get a soothing playlist. We always entertain suggestions for a B&B-friendly breakfast playlist that will make just about everybody happy.

Background Noise Level

An article from Noisy Planet talks about how stressful it is to be in a loud restaurant. If you stop to think about it, you can see the underlying rationale behind the noisy breakfast room in a chain hotel. The management wants to stress the customers out enough so that they will leave quickly and not hang around the premises.

A blaring TV announcer talking at slightly above conversational volume about how you are in imminent danger is just the thing to push you into your car in a hurry.

At our place, we try to create the opposite effect. We want you to stay, enjoy pleasant conversation if you like, or soak up some peace and quiet if that's your preference. If you linger all day, that's fine with us. Our breakfast room has been set up to delight our guests, not drive them away.

Sights

Colors

I suppose sight falls into two categories: colors and visual interest. There is even some science devoted to the selection of color schemes. An article from *This Old House* suggests that you can use colors to give drama to a room. Some of the images the article uses to illustrate that point are beautiful and depend on the furnishings, of course, but we are resisting the idea of drama. Instead, we're striving for welcoming simplicity.

An even better article from sleep.com says that you should consider yellow (as in orange juice), green, and coral as your basic colors because they are so soothing. As it turns out, we did not need to spend too much energy or money to set up a breakfast room with a yellow and coral theme because ours was already decorated that way. The lovely breakfast setting below from our kitchen seating area has all the required elements. It looks as though we stumbled onto the truth. I guess eggs and orange juice are yellow, right?

Visual Interest

We will talk more about visual interest when we start describing the food presentation itself. However, setting up a breakfast room also requires maintaining visual interest in the surroundings to entertain your guests, however briefly. At The Firefly, there are little areas throughout the building that are set up to give visual interest. The little space on the kitchen counter in the photo below was set up to be eye-catching and convey a welcoming image. We're constantly trying to probe the boundary between visually interesting and cluttered. It's a fine line.

Feelings: Ambient Light and Temperature

When thinking about light and temperature, there are a few things to keep in mind. The most important is to ask yourself, "When does the sun come up?" The time when the sun comes up is the very definition of predictability. You did know, didn't you, that the date of the latest sunrise in the northern hemisphere is December 7? Because of our location in Georgia, our latest sunrise time in December is 7:30 AM. We're lucky in that regard. Depending on the time you like to get up, you never really need to eat breakfast in the dark.

Sidebar: For some of us, getting up at 7:30 is the definition of sleeping in. We are more accustomed to getting up at 6:22 AM or before, which is the earliest sunrise of the year for us. It happens on June 19 each year.

Aside from brighter mornings in the winter, we're also lucky since it never gets that cold around here, although the mornings quite often have some cloud cover. So for us, we tried to make the most of our filtered winter sunshine as we set up the breakfast room. What all of this means for our guests is that, by breakfast time, it will be daylight and warm enough to be comfortable. Even in the winter, it still won't be terrible.

We can't say the same for our northern neighbors. In Fargo, it can be cold and dark at breakfast time. If I wanted to set up a breakfast room at a B&B in a place like Fargo, I might have some serious lighting and temperature issues to consider. This otherwise lovely place has an average temperature of minus-2F at 7:00 AM in January with sunrise as late as 8:30 AM, thanks to its location so far north and in the western part of the central time zone.

Outdoor Seating

If you set up a breakfast room indoors, it's good to know what kind of lighting you have and how much you'll need. At The Firefly, it is usually reasonably nice during our peak B&B season, so it makes sense to provide outdoor seating too.

Fire and Water

Fast Casual Magazine makes a case for using outdoor seating as a way to increase capacity in restaurants. This is because both fire and water appeal to the customers' attraction to nature. There are no statistics on what fraction of restaurants or bed and breakfast establishments have the space for outdoor seating. However, we at The Firefly are lucky in that there are several places where we have been able to create pleasant outdoor breakfast experiences.

We have a big porch attached to the front of the house that overlooks half an acre of lawn space. The sun peeks around the corner of the building toward the end of breakfast. At certain times of the year, this is a good thing.

We also have a large brick patio, underutilized at the moment, that could be converted to a breakfast space. This is a quiet area that overlooks our water garden.

Potentially, there is a third place, but it is mainly intended for the occupant of the "Treehouse Room." One of our rooms has a large wooden deck that overlooks about two acres of woodland. If the guests in that room chose to take their breakfast back there and sit out on the deck to commune with nature, that would also be fine with us.

Alternative Indoor Seating

We have a couple of pleasant breakfast-friendly spots inside our B&B. There is a big sunroom that overlooks the backyard. It's a very nice space for breakfast and has become a favorite of some guests.

This room has several of the advantages of the outdoor breakfast area in that it overlooks the backyard with a view of the water feature. It is also bug-free. We talked about the fact that the mild temperature and plentiful daylight encourage sitting outside at our place. A not-so-pleasant feature toward the end of the summer is the abundance of flies. As the temperatures tend to get sticky at this time of year, some guests are more comfortable in the air-conditioned interior than in the great outdoors. For these reasons, we've found that guests favor gathering in our big kitchen even though it is on the dark side of the house in the mornings.

In the evening, this beautiful, well-lit spot has also been known to attract the adult beverage crowd. Although visitors are encouraged to circulate elsewhere, the tendency is to hang out in the kitchen because the vibe is better. There is actually a perfectly nice room with a fireplace and comfortable seating, but the guests tend not to like it as well as the kitchen.

The Kitchen as the Heart of the House

National Public Radio published an article recently on the topic of why people gather in the kitchen. The article talks about several reasons for this, including "messy informality." It basically says what we've already learned at The Firefly. Our guests tend to gravitate to the kitchen whenever they can.

The Joanna Gaines idea of opening the kitchen up to the living room for entertaining is not happening at our place because we want to stay true to the 1939 spirit of the house. Its kitchen was built to be the gathering point. So far, that concept seems to be working just fine for us. Plus, the kitchen is conveniently close to the little downstairs bathroom.

Buffet-Style Dining

There is a school of thought that says that a buffet is a simple way to let guests help themselves a little. We found a concept for a breakfast island on YouTube that has a lot of similarities to our space and includes a three-level breakfast island that lets the guests graze if they want.

This is very elaborate, and I only mention it as an idea. You could, if sufficiently motivated, set up a pretty little breakfast bar with a few dollars and a power drill.

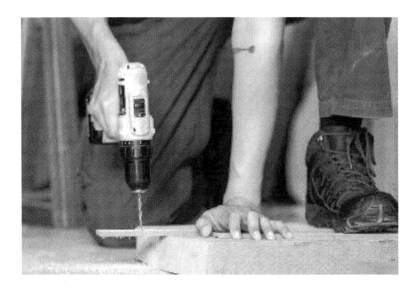

If the crowd is big enough, we will deviate from single servings and go to buffet-style dining. However, for the most part, breakfast is lovingly, individually prepared by the Earth Goddess. What we don't want to duplicate is something like the chain hotel assembly line breakfast.

Despite all of the design work and engineering, the breakfast feeding in the next photo was designed by a committee for efficiency.

How many times have you been to a chain hotel, wanted badly for those beautiful bagels to be good, but had them turn out to be dry and annoying?

The Place Setting

You have to kind of chuckle at the idea of the "correct" table setting. I like the white glove approach and thumb distance from the edge of the table in the next photo.

You can get an idea of the way it is actually done at our place from some of the photos in earlier chapters. We like to be casual and welcoming. If you need to stay at a more formal place, we can find one for you. The salt, pepper, and butter (as local as possible) are available on the table, along with beautiful napkins. (Coral and green, remember?)

Of course, all of this varies with the whim of the Earth Goddess, and variety is good. Go with it. The table in the photo is usually in the kitchen, but it has been known to move between the sunroom, patio, and even to the studio room in the back more recently.

Mingling

There is a bell curve on wakeup times. A few guests like to get up early, especially Europeans who are still functioning on their local time. A few guests get up late, especially Californians who are about equally jetlagged from the opposite coast. We book groups from a local consultant who conducts executive training. They sometimes arrive for breakfast together and talk about what is happening in their class that day.

The B&B atmosphere encourages mingling at breakfast. Unlike the local chain hotel, we look at the conversational atmosphere as an important part of the customer experience. An article in bedandbreakfast.com says that the breakfast interaction among guests should be viewed as part of the B&B adventure.

We at The Firefly want to encourage you to have fun interacting with your fellow travelers. You never know what you might learn. We have an abundance of information about the local area, including events, directions, and things to do and see. Breakfast is an easy place to plan your day, and it is always helpful to get advice from a knowledgeable host.

Taking It Back to the Room

At this point, I should say a word about solitary dining. Some guests like the option of either cooking their own breakfast in their room or taking some food back to their rooms to get ready for the day. We are perfectly fine with these alternatives and support anybody starting their day this way.

An article in *Forbes Magazine* named dining alone as a growing trend. Although the article is a bit dated, it is probably accurate to say that the trend continues. Very nearly half of all adult eating activities are done alone.

There are plenty of reasons for this practice and plenty of consequences, including overeating, snackification (in which a series of snacks substitutes for meals), and hurrying through meals. At The Firefly, we have a positive attitude toward health, and that includes mental health. We want to give our guests plenty of opportunities to reach out and connect with others. For the most part, we encourage eating as a group.

Breakfast Room Lessons

In our quest for setting up the ideal atmosphere for a delightful breakfast experience, we have been guided by a few simple principles:

1. Pay attention to the senses.
2. Make the guests comfortable in an informal and welcoming way.
3. Set up the dining area pleasantly.
4. Let the guests be who they are.
5. Work with what you have.

None of these concepts are especially complicated. In our case, setting up a breakfast room takes advantage of the natural beauty and layout of our little house, as odd as it is. The result is a pleasant and welcoming experience that gets our guests on their way about their business and makes their stay with us memorable.

5 – Wake Up and Smell the Coffee

Now that we've spent some time describing all the spaces where a guest can take breakfast at The Firefly, it's time to move on to the subject of the meal itself. But before we get to a discussion of the specific dishes on the menu, our guests still have to rise and shine.

Wakeup Proverbs

Okay, assuming that you've gotten here and enjoyed a good night's rest (or the "bed" component of a bed and breakfast), you need to wake up the following morning before you can savor the "breakfast" part of the name. Here are some motivational proverbs to get you started:

- **Some of us wake up. Others roll over.** *(Mark Twight)*
- **Wake up to find out that you are the eyes of the world.** *(Robert Hunter)*
- **Wake up this morning knowing that the possibility for love is closer.** *(Jon Jones)*

Here are some of our own local wakeup proverbs:

- **Wake up and feed me.** (*Posh and the Cats*)
- **Cluck, Cluck.** (*The Chickens*)

Make up your own. If you give us one that's clever enough, we might make a sign and hang it up someplace.

Wake Up and Smell the Coffee

The expression "wake up and smell the coffee" has been around for a long time. It doesn't generally have a positive meaning. This odd phrase is almost always used derisively as if the recipient has been missing out on some form of enlightenment.

When we say "wake up and smell the coffee" at the Firefly, it is intended to be a good thing. The Earth Goddess has a little coffee grinder and makes her morning brew in a French press.

You might find fresh dairy products, butter, or any number of other coffee condiments available to make yours the way you want it. Flavorless coffee is available locally if that suits you better.

Have It Your Way

The individual guest rooms in the guest house each have a microwave as well as access to some microwaveable coffee. Many of the guests like to exercise the option of privacy in the morning. The porch of the Treehouse Room is particularly pleasant early in the day because the sun shines down on it. So, if you want to get your own breakfast treat during your travels and keep it in your fridge, the Earth Goddess is happy with that and won't mind.

6 – Breakfast Unchained

Now that you've had your coffee and are at least slightly awake let's talk about the importance of breakfast. You've probably heard that breakfast is the most important meal of the day, but nobody really explains why that is. You're about to get the whole story.

Breakfast Health Bonus

Part of the importance of breakfast is that it wakes up the brain. Nutritionists advise a breakfast that contains between 20-35% of your daily caloric intake within two hours of waking up. This is because breakfast restores cognitive function (aka thinking) by increasing blood sugar levels early in the day.

According to Rush University, people who eat breakfast tend to consume less food overall during the day. They also tend to have a lower body mass index (BMI) than people who skip breakfast. On the minus side, avoiding breakfast comes with a higher incidence of heart problems. People who skip breakfast are 87% more likely to have a cardiovascular event than those who eat breakfast every day.

A Good Breakfast Jump Starts Your Day

Some of our guests have projects to complete in the area. Invariably, they report that even a small breakfast of coffee and one of our simple foods helps them get off to a good start. So, to sum it all up, we make breakfast for our guests because we like them and want them to be healthy and alert for whatever they have going on that day.

Breakfast Brings People Together

No less of an authority than bedandbreakfast.com says that meeting the host and mingling with the other guests is a major reason why people stay at a B&B. Part of the B&B experience involves engaging with people from different parts of the world. About 40% of the guests at The Firefly come from outside North America. They are curious about local ways in the southeastern United States. A traditional breakfast is part of their immersive American experience.

Aside from our foreign clientele, many of our B&B guests are solo travelers. They may be touring our part of the country or staying at our place as part of a local visit. Solo travelers often like to learn things about the region from the other guests. The morning meal is a great place for them to get travel tips and find help in planning their day.

Breakfast Establishes a Connection

From the point of view of the host, breakfast is the time of day when we have the most opportunity to interact with our guests. In addition to sharing stories and appreciating one another's lifestyle, taking a few minutes to get the guest's story is an important form of information exchange. The innkeeper wants to know how the guest's stay is going. In an effort to keep our guests comfortable, we need to know if there are any issues that have to be addressed.

From the point of view of the guest, mingling at breakfast is an opportunity to tell their story to the other guests and exchange notes with them. They are likely to hear something interesting. According to muchneeded.com, Airbnb guests differ from the general public. They tend to be younger, better educated, and are more likely to be female than male. All of these qualities lead to stimulating table talk and make for a unique experience for all concerned.

We want our guests to feel as if they are sharing their entire travel adventure with us. We like to think that we change the lives of every new guest, just a little. Likewise, every new guest changes our place a little too. They contribute to the spirit of The Firefly by connecting with the place itself and with their fellow guests.

Breakfast Helps Guests Relax

Let me give you an example of the opposite of a relaxing experience when you're traveling. You roll out of bed as the alarm rings. Then, you stumble around in the dark in a strange place because you're cognitively impaired. After that, you drive into town and navigate your way to the closest fast-food restaurant and/or Waffle House. (Well, to be perfectly honest, everyone should go to a Waffle House at least once just to say they've done it.)

Instead, particularly if The Firefly is your destination, you might find it better to start your day in less of a rush. Part of the motivation for staying at a B&B is to reduce the number of things you need to worry about first thing in the morning. The whole point of serving breakfast at a B&B is to encourage guests to start their day gently.

Breakfast Gives Early Risers an Edge

Aside from those who prefer a gentle start to the day, there are also other types of B&B guests. They operate on an entirely different schedule by using the hours between 5:00 AM and 8:00 AM productively to work on blog posts, projects, planning for the day, and exercise. If you are one of those people, you probably already know the value of a little extra time in the morning. You should couple that jumpstart with some high brain-power food before you blast into the world, ready to accomplish something. We can certainly accommodate that type of guest as well.

Breakfast Customizes the Guest Experience

Breakfast can be used as a way to tailor the B&B experience to the individual needs of the guest. This makes each stay unique and a one-of-a-kind experience for each visitor. People who are adventurous by nature tend to seek out variety. As it happens, this quest for variety has important psychological implications. According to researchers at Columbia University, if people are confined to a narrow space in a store and given few selections to choose from, they tend to feel threatened. They perceive that their freedom has been curtailed in some way. It stands to reason that the opposite is true too. By giving guests customized breakfast options, we appeal to their need for variety and reinforce their sense of freedom.

The Chain Hotel Experience Versus the Delightful Experience

Unlike the uniqueness of a B&B, the chain hotel experience is all about standardization. People who travel frequently on business have stories about waking up in a hotel room not knowing what city, or which room, they are in. They forgot where they parked their car. Their breakfast experience is deliberately standardized too. There is an underlying reason for that conformity—quality assurance.

Unlike the adventurous types who tend to stay at B&Bs, there are some people who thrive on standardization. Such people look at predictability as a way to enhance their sense of control. They are more likely to trust a hotel chain that is known for its uniform appearance. In the B&B experience, guests give away a little of their control in exchange for learning and stimulation.

One of the downsides of uniformity is that it reduces a guest's chances of having a surprising experience that might turn out to be delightful. A big part of our job as B&B hosts is to give you some measure of predictability while, at the same time, offering a certain amount of uniqueness that will stay with you on your path forward. A breakfast experience that isn't completely standardized is an important part of creating that effect. The B&B host tries to skillfully manage the guest experience by understanding and adapting to guest needs while at the same time providing them with some pleasant surprises.

GOES WELL WITH GRITS

An Exceptional Breakfast Can Make a B&B Stay Memorable

During our travels as B&B guests, we once stayed at a very pretty bed and breakfast in North Carolina. It was convenient to the activities we had planned at the time and was close to some little restaurants and a small college. The innkeepers, however, were the most memorable part of the experience for us, much more so than the room itself. The lady of the house was a trained chef. In the few days that we visited, we had some wonderful, individually prepared three-course breakfasts. Among other things, we feasted on omelets and pear pastry, with each meal nicely served on a white tablecloth.

This gourmet breakfast was included with the stay at no extra charge. We didn't miss a standard McBreakfast in the least. Our experience won't be repeated in exactly that same way because it can't be. If you stay at a chain hotel, their policy of predictability will give you exactly what you expect to get and no better. At the North Carolina B&B, we got much better than what we expected. Breakfast became the key feature of our stay at this place because the meals offered a high-end experience in an unexpected place.

The importance of breakfast as part of the B&B experience can't be overemphasized. It makes sense for us, as hosts, to give this important meal some thoughtful planning. We set the scene, prepare good food, lay down some expectations of uniqueness, and the result is a delightful experience for our guests.

7 – Ten Simple Facts About Pancakes

Scene: A Stone Age Conversation

Date and Time: 3500 BCE at About 8:00 AM

Location: Italian Alps

WAIT PERSON: Sit wherever you like, Hun.

OTZI: *(Winces and slouches into a seat.)* Thanks. Do you have any coffee?

WAIT PERSON: Coffee? Never heard of it. All we have is barley soaked in water. We call it "Bob Water."

OTZI: Bob water?

WAIT PERSON: Yeah, he invented it. He soaks some little green flowers in it to make it spicy.

OTZI: *(Sipping.)* I suppose it might grow on you. Do you have any food?

WAIT PERSON: Yeah. We have barley soaked in water and then cooked. We flavor the concoction up with a little honey. We call them "Bob Cakes."

OTZI: Same Bob?

WAIT PERSON: No, that was Bob the Baker. He invented Bob Cakes. Bob the Brewer invented Bob Water. All the men in this village are named Bob. There are not many of us. We know which Bob invented what.

(In a few minutes, some Bob Cakes appear. Otzi samples one, makes a bit of a face, and then slowly eats the rest.)

WAIT PERSON: What do you think?

OTZI: Edible. I am headed north today and glad to get anything to eat.

WAIT PERSON: Oh, up into the hills? I'd be careful if I were you. A snowstorm can come up out of nowhere at this time of year. If you ever fell down one of those crevasses, there's no telling how long it would take for someone to find you.

OTZI: I'll keep that in mind.

(He gathers his shawl around his shoulders and limps to the door.)

OTZI: Thanks for breakfast. Tell Bob, good job on the Bob Water. It's making me a little lightheaded.

Simple Fact #1: Pancakes Are Ancient

Pancakes have been around for a very long time. They were found in the cold, frozen stomach of Otzi, the Iceman who fell into a glacier 5,500 years ago. We know this because the ice preserved his body perfectly.

The way he died raises a lot of questions about Otzi. Did the carb rush he got that morning distract him enough so that he slipped off the glacier? Did he make his own pancakes, or did his mom make them? What kind of pancake would be recognizable 5,500 years from now if the same thing happened to us?

Simple Fact #2: People Prefer Pancakes Over Bacon (in Milwaukee)

According to a recent survey, pancakes are more popular than bacon as a breakfast food. In addition, we discovered that there is now such a thing as a "second breakfast" because people tend to rush through "first breakfast" so that they can get out the door. When they starve out by 10:30 AM, they need to forage for food. If you were in the bread business, this would be vital information. Also true, I suppose, if you were in the bacon business.

Simple Fact #3: Pancakes Require Some Skill to Prepare

The inability to make pancakes was a running joke on Green Acres. Millennials take note: This was a show from the Stone Age of TV. The plot involved city people who got the crazy notion of moving out into the country to take up farming. One of the co-stars of the show was Bea Benaderet. She also played Jethro's mom (Cousin Pearl) on the Beverly Hillbillies; Kate, the proprietor of the Shady Rest Hotel (from Petticoat Junction); and the voice of Betty Rubble on the Flintstones. You will probably have to be a baby boomer to know or care about any of those bits of trivia.

Simple Fact #4: Pancakes Are Not Terrible for You (Although They Do Contain a Lot of Carbs)

Here's the nutritional breakdown for a cup of Hungry Jack pancake mix:

Total Fat – 1 gram

Sodium – 480 mg

Total Carbohydrate – 39 grams

Total Calories – 450

Percent of Calories as Fat – 8.8%

Percent of Calories as Protein – 10.4%

Percent of Calories as Carbohydrate – 80.8%

There are a couple of points to keep in mind about this information. First of all, the data is given for one cup of dry mix. You usually mix the dry powder with about 2/3 cup of water, and no one eats a bowl full of pancakes. So, assuming you only ate half a bowl full of pancakes, you would only be getting 225 calories for breakfast. That really isn't all that high. If you add a slice of butter (102 calories) and two tablespoons of maple syrup (another 104 calories), you're still under 500 calories for the morning. Of course, whether this is a healthy meal or not depends a lot on what you do afterward.

If you go out and sit in an office all day, this type of breakfast will probably not be good for you. If you go out and try to walk across a glacier, and/or hack out 36 feet of concrete (like we did the other day), pancakes for breakfast probably won't hurt you.

Simple Fact #5: There Is an International House of Them

Ah, IHOP. It was founded in 1958, which was at the beginning of the interstate highway system. This company brought two things to the world. The first was standardization. Back in the Stone Age of the greasy spoon roadside diner, you never knew exactly what you were going to get when you ordered pancakes. So, thanks to IHOP, you knew what you were going to get— standardized mediocre pancakes. (As you know, at The Firefly, we have a hard time appreciating standardization.)

The second innovation introduced by IHOP was the elimination of closing time. Because the chain was open 24 hours, you could wander into one of their restaurants after what used to be the traditional "closing time."

In some regions of the country, doing this is considered an important part of a college education. Eating breakfast in the middle of the night comes with a few unpleasant side effects.

For starters, it will give you a greasy, stomach-unsettling meal right before bedtime. It will also expose you to the kind of workforce that you do not want to join—the night waitstaff at the IHOP.

NOTE: Not that waiting tables at IHOP is not a respectable position in life, but you can likely find a more desirable job for more money if you pay attention in calculus class.

Revisionist Thinking

Do you remember a few years ago when they tried to change the name of IHOP to the International House of Breakfast (IHOB)? The negative reaction from the public was so overwhelming that it became one of those brilliant marketing ideas that backfired. In the end, it did teach a valuable lesson. IHOB reverted back to IHOP, proving that change is not always a good thing. It didn't work for soft drinks, and it doesn't work for pancakes either.

Simple Fact #6: People Still Like Eating Them

According to an article in foodmanufacturing.com, 60% of households still use packaged pancake mix, presumably to mix pancakes instead of waffles. This is despite the various trends toward gluten-free, low carb, and generally highly portable food that you can cram into your life as you sit behind the wheel of your Hyundai.

This high statistic on pancake consumption is curious because, depending on your point of view, slowing down to make pancakes could be considered a pain point. A pain point is an incremental complication that will clog up your day.

So, there may be some underlying value in the friendly, round shape of warm, cooked flour and water looking up at you in the morning. At The Firefly, pancakes are not considered painful. We're trying to do away with pain points for our guests.

Simple Fact #7: Scratch Is Not Really Much Better Than Box Mix

Okay, there may be some disagreement on this topic. The question always comes up whether pancakes are best prepared from scratch or from a box mix. In a test conducted by bonappetit.com, kids and gentlemen in a hurry were indifferent. Foodies could tell the difference, as could little old ladies. I suppose the taste is dependent on how much syrup and butter you put on the pancakes.

An article in huffpost.com points out some questionable ingredients in the box mix variety. In addition to the normal enriched flour, you also get a dose of partially hydrogenated vegetable oil, aka trans fat. So, it might make some sense nutritionally to limit your consumption of the box mix product.

It also makes a difference how often you eat pancakes. If you ate nothing but pancakes all the time, trans fat consumption might be an important problem for you. Eating box mix pancakes once in a blue moon, whenever you stop off at some pleasant B&B, is probably not an issue compared to the other ways you might be ingesting trans fats.

Simple Fact #8: It's All About the Toppings

Is it not true, in your heart of hearts, that pancakes are all about the toppings? Do you really want to carry one of these things around in a baggie to snack on all day? Maybe pancakes are really all about the nice warm feeling and bright colors of the sweet and syrupy toppings that you put on them, and not about the pancakes themselves.

This is worthy of an experiment. Take some pancakes and plop them down in front of someone without any toppings. Then take a cupful of toppings and plop that down in front of someone. Then, take both the pancakes and toppings and plop the combination down in front of your test subject. Seems like the pancakes, as a delivery device for something else, would be the winner.

Simple Fact #9: Waffles Versus Pancakes

According to a survey of Twitter users, there is a 2:1 preference for waffles among this not-widespread demographic. Surprisingly, this topic is a matter of heated debate.

The most commonly given advantage of waffles over pancakes is the little grid pattern, which holds more syrup and butter. Those who fail to see that as an advantage push their argument for pancakes as the better option. Because this is such a fraught issue among breakfast aficionados, we might try surveying our readers on the question. If you have a preference for one over the other, please feel free to let us know your views.

Simple Fact 10: The Firefly Pancake Recipe

Here is our version of this ever-popular breakfast dish:

    1 cup almond flour
    1 cup coconut flour
    1/4 cup erythritol
    4 teaspoons baking powder
    1/4 teaspoon baking soda
    1 1/2 cups flax or almond milk
    1/4 cup butter, melted (from Farmview Market)
    2 teaspoons vanilla
    1 large egg (preferably recently laid by a chicken that has foraged for food around the farm).

Combine in a mixing bowl while making small talk in a large country kitchen. Drop into funny shapes onto an electric griddle. The preferred griddle lube shall be butter.

Food for thought: Does it matter if you are cooking this on an electric griddle versus cast iron or something earth-friendly?

According to the Earth Goddess, the electric griddle is favored for quantity, but the cast iron gives you crispy edges. Also, a thinner version can be made for crepes and a thicker version for bread. Serving suggestion: Top off with a mastodon steak. The Earth Goddess has not offered a suggestion as to who will be killing the mastodon.

8 – House Waffles Versus the Waffle House

<u>The Origin of Waffles</u>

There is much confusion about whether the word "waffle" is a noun or a verb. In the noun form, a waffle is a cakelike batter cooked between two hot metal plates.

The verb "waffle" means to express a firm commitment about something and then assert that commitment with less certainty later on. Ironically, that is the opposite of what happens to an actual waffle, which gets construction-grade hard the longer it sits around.

Originally, the Greeks cooked thin cakes between two flat pieces of metal over an open fire. These were called *obleios*, or wafers. A later version, *oublies*, emerged during the Middle Ages, when the otherwise minimally edible concoction started to be mixed with fun ingredients, such as wine and cheese.

Low Country Waffles

According to Wikipedia, waffles, as we now know them, became popular in the low countries of Belgium and the Netherlands. This famous breakfast item emerged at the same time as pressed communion wafers. In a way, this is the answer to the unanswerable question, "Why would someone expend energy to press otherwise good bread between metal plates just to make a pattern out of them when metal molds are so hard to make?"

The modern version of waffles apparently evolved in the 16th century, when the classic grid waffle iron emerged, along with a recipe that consisted of flour, egg, and sugar. By the 18th century, when sugar and iron became cheap commodities, waffles came within reach of ordinary citizens.

The Waffle House

Speaking of ordinary citizens, we had a conversation about waffles for the masses just the other day. A road trip to the Waffle House is still on our agenda. Oddly, waffles are not the most popular item on the menu at this restaurant, which is mainly found in the southeastern United States. Despite the name, the Waffle House is not about waffles.

Waffles are actually the fifth most popular item on the Waffle House menu. Egg dishes must be in much higher demand because the restaurant chain consumes 2% of our nation's egg output. Despite their apparent indifference to serving waffles in the actual restaurant, the company is doing well at marketing its custom-blended waffle mix. This product sells for $8.00 per box, and each box makes about 15 to 18 waffles.

NOTE: If you order waffles at the International House of Pancakes, you will be asked to leave.

The Difference Between Pancakes and Waffles

According to the Hungry Jack company, producers of pancake mix, you can alter their recipe to make waffles by adding ¼ cup of Crisco Oil and one egg. These are the ingredients you would need to add to a normal double batch of pancakes to turn them into waffle mix. For your trouble, you will get 12 four-by-four-inch waffles. That translates to three heats of your old-timey waffle iron.

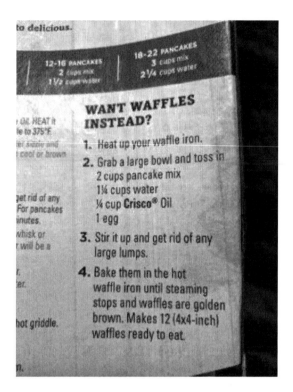

Alton Brown, celebrity chef, takes a different view of the proper way to adapt pancake mix for waffles. He believes that the critical difference between pancake and waffle mix is the addition of sugar because it increases caramelization and creates a crispy exterior. This is the reason why waffles hold up better than pancakes when drenched with toppings. What that information should tell you is that the Hungry Jack commercial pancake mix contains plenty of sugar as it is. (You might have been able to predict that.)

Whole Wheat

The presence of "whole wheat" anything would cause it to be thrown out of a Waffle House chain restaurant in favor of the prefabricated mix that came from corporate. (There is no telling how many waffles you will get if you start with nearly 10 cups of flour, but it is likely that you are hosting a party.)

Waffle Iron Lubrication

This is an important topic that deserves some attention. What is the best lubrication for your waffle iron? Since a waffle has a rather complex shape, getting your waffle to release from the waffle iron is a difficult task. Most recipes call for some kind of oil or butter to be applied to the mold. The question is, "Does the lubrication add or detract from the waffle's flavor?"

The Greeks chose to use olive oil. Most modern recipes call for spraying the iron thoroughly with Pam, which is artificially flavored soybean oil. If you have a religious objection to soybean oil, you may want to adjust your method.

Should You Throw Out the First Waffle?

You might have heard the advice that you should always throw away the first waffle of the day that comes out of your waffle iron. There are several reasons for this:

- Oil and food particles left over from the previous use need to be removed.
- The waffle iron needs one complete heat cycle to come up to the proper temperature.
- The surface of the waffle iron needs to be conditioned.

There are plenty of opinions regarding this throwaway waffle conundrum. Keep in mind, per the above calculation, that if you choose to throw out the first waffle, this will be literally one-third of your batch. Yahoo Answers states that the first waffle is "usually" a throwaway, but the source does not proscribe this action.

Waffle Throwing

The unusual practice of throwing waffles onto the ice at a hockey game is not recommended. A man in Toronto ended up in jail for doing so. Of course, this occurred in Canada, where hockey is more precious than waffles. Since the modern waffle has a disklike shape, the temptation might be to use it in a contest. A Google search did not reveal any sort of waffle-throwing championship in America. This means that we can host one if we wish and finally find a use for that first throwaway waffle from the day's batch.

Waffle-Eating Contests

Although there are no waffle throwing competitions, there are championships for waffle eating.

At the San Jose Barracuda Waffle-Eating Contest, Joey Chestnut, a professional eater, ate 81 waffles in eight minutes. This fellow has won multiple Nathan's Famous hot dog eating contests too. The Waffle House also sponsors a waffle-eating contest through an organization called "Major League Eating," to which we can just shake our heads.

The International House of Waffles

A Google search on the topic of a waffle counterpart for IHOP did not turn up much. Evidently, IHOP considers this phrase to be part of its trademark. That fact doesn't prevent people from trying to use it, though. There is, or was, an International House of Waffles in Potsdam, New York. There was another somewhere in California and a third in Belgium, slightly beyond the reach of American lawyers.

Eggos

The Kellogg Company is the inventor of the Eggo "waffle." This is a pre-made, packaged frozen waffle that you can drop into a toaster just in case you don't like toast. Like all mass-produced food items, Eggos taste nondescript because they are engineered that way. They're formulated so that the largest possible number of people won't utterly hate them. To us, they taste slightly worse than they might because of the massive advertising campaign that first introduced them.

Chain Hotel Waffles

Have you seen one of those waffle machines they have over at the Hampton Inn? Here is how it works. You dispense a little cupful of batter from the batter machine. Presumably, the batter comes pre-mixed from somewhere. The waffle iron stays hot all the time. You pour your batter into the waffle iron and wait. When it is ready, the machine beeps, and your lovely waffle comes out.

There is another type of commercial waffle machine that makes you flip your food over for some reason, and the waffle comes out upside down. The advantage, if you want to call it that, is that you, the guest, provide all the free labor of preparing your own breakfast. Does this seem right to you? Does putting you to work before coffee enhance your breakfast experience?

To tell the honest truth, even as a guest, you are probably more efficient than 90% of the commercial cooks in the United States. Aside from contributing free labor, you are also benefiting the chain hotel by cutting down on waste. The hotel can't predict how many waffles they're going to need in a typical day. With you as the chef and consumer, they don't need to know.

There are some obvious problems with this system, though. Who knows where the batter came from and what is in it? Do they recycle the leftover batter on the following day? Do they, or do they not, throw out the first waffle of the morning? What, if anything, is used as the lube for the waffle iron?

The biggest problem, of course, is that this waffle contraption is usually being operated by some giggling 15-year-old on a choir trip. These young people are not known for their problem-solving abilities. If you want to get your breakfast and hit the road, you have to wait for the adolescents to run through a few cycles of failure before they get their waffles. You're better off choosing the hard-boiled eggs. With regard to the question of quality, I will entertain opinions on whether these hotel waffles are better than or not as good as "real waffles" made by a crazy aunt.

B&B Waffle Rules

Here is how it works at our B&B:

- The guest does not have to mix, cook, and prepare their own.
- Fresh eggs from the Earth Goddess's chickens are used if there are any.
- The waffle iron is modern non-stick Belgian-American style.
- Coconut oil is sprayed on the surface after every heat.
- The first waffle is eaten by the Earth Goddess (to make sure they're good).
- They are too good to throw. This is what we love about serving waffles.
- The recipe is variable, like everything else. No two days are exactly the same.
- Flavors such as chai, cinnamon, peanut butter, or any other fruit are thrown in just for fun.

Different Types of Waffles

Oddly enough, a very good article explaining the different types of waffles is presented by the people who sell waffle machines. Who knew that there are a half dozen types of waffles, and some include yeast for extra leavening and fluffiness? I think the Waffle House probably just sells waffles. (This is because the Waffle House is not about waffles.)

The cooking surface is also a variable. The choices of metal are iron, cast iron, aluminum, or some combination of alloys. Teflon or ceramic release agent? There is a lunatic fringe that has an opinion on that topic too. This is because of some sort of perceived health impairment.

Antique Waffles Like Your Crazy Aunt Used to Make

If you are opinionated on the issue of the proper cooking surface, you may spend between $20 and $50 to buy an authentic 1945-55 electric waffle iron. This might be because you literally want to have one like Grandma used to have before she threw hers out and bought a new one from China.

The vintage appliance might be considered slightly more wholesome than the modern version. But if you use an antique waffle iron, it makes more sense to throw out the first waffle of the day. You don't know what's been stuck to the grid for the past 70 years.

Option 1: Keto Waffles

This recipe comes from Skinny Fitalicious:

- 2 large eggs
- ¼ cup unsweetened almond milk plus 2 tbsp unsweetened almond milk
- ¼ cup coconut flour
- ½ tsp baking powder
- 1 tsp cinnamon

Option 2: More Keto Waffles

This recipe comes from Gimme Delicious:

- 4 large eggs
- 4 oz cream cheese (½ block)
- ½ cup almond flour
- 2 tbsp melted butter or coconut oil
- 1 tsp vanilla extract
- 1 tbsp erythritol (optional)
- 1 tsp baking powder

Option 3: Traditional Waffles

This non-keto recipe comes from Martha Stewart:

- 1 cup all-purpose flour
- 2 tbsp sugar
- 1 tsp baking powder
- ¼ tsp salt
- 1 cup milk
- 2 large eggs
- 4 tbsp (1/2 stick) unsalted butter
- Toppings (See Below)

Do you get the idea that you should start with a couple of eggs? You have sugar options, including omitting it in favor of erythritol if you like. Use some type of flour (almond maybe) and then a little salt.

Toppings

At The Firefly, waffles are mainly about the toppings. What we love about serving waffles is that we have a source for fresh berries from the local producers. There are local peaches and apples from within 100 miles of our place too. Pecans or nuts may be available, depending on the season. You can also find locally produced molasses and syrup produced by a human. (This is because we like humans.)

Waffles are a little adventure at our place. We are not quite earth-friendly enough to serve raw, unhomogenized milk, but there is some to be found in the area. Unfortunately, the FDA and the state inspectors do not appreciate raw dairy products in the way that the permaculture people do.

NOTE: Permaculture is the practice of creating a self-sustaining agricultural ecosystem that doesn't harm the environment.

That Waffle Feeling

What we love best about serving waffles is that it is done in a room full of happy people. There will be the aroma of freshly brewed coffee and maybe some sizzling bacon. There might be some sort of easy-listening music because it's still early in the morning. A dog might bark. Chickens might be walking around, and cats may be wrestling. I guess what I am trying to say is that waffles are more of a feeling than a food.

9 – The Strange Origins of Cereal for Breakfast

Scene: Speaking of Cereal

Place and Time: In the Car at 8:00 AM
Location: Covington, Georgia

A: *(Sniffing.)* What's that?
B: What's that what?

A: The smell. Something's cooking.
B: Yeah, that's Cheerios. Wheaties day is Friday.

A: They make Cheerios here?
B: Yeah.

A: I thought Cheerios are made of oats. There aren't any oats around here.
B: Yeah, I know. But Cheerios also have a lot of sugar, and there is no sugar around here either. General Mills has no problem trucking all of this stuff in. Actually, they might have rail cars.

A: Why don't they make this stuff close to the oats?

B: Because they did some kind of calculation that says it's cheaper for them to locate close to the consumer. It's all about transportation. I imagine it's more expensive to ship a box of Cheerios than it is to ship tanker cars or trucks of either oats or sugar.

A: All of that shipping is bad, you know. It's a supply chain.

B: To the company, it's cheaper and better. Plus, they have land costs and energy costs, and they need to hire a labor force. All of that must be cheap here, or they would make their cereal somewhere else.

A: But what if there is a disruption? What if there are transportation problems or problems with the labor force?

(Ominous silence.)

Cereal for Big Families and B&Bs

There are plenty of similarities between feeding guests at a small B&B and trying to feed a big family. Both have cost considerations, a convenience factor, and you want to make some effort to enhance the experience and make it memorable in a positive way.

Not too long ago, it was a quaint idea to have lots of kids as long as you were able to feed them. These days, according to nokidhungry.org, two-thirds of the kids in this country either don't get fed breakfast or else skip it deliberately. We've already talked about the physical and intellectual problems of failing to fuel up in the morning. It's bad enough when adults do this, but kids ought to be taught better habits to give them a fighting chance in life. Sorry, this is a bit of a downer. (We are all about reality.)

So, everything that follows in this chapter is predicated on the archaic Walton/Douglas/Brady Bunch theory that a big, well-cared-for family is fine. For a big family or a small B&B, breakfast is an important part of the experience. Parents out there in the imaginary, wholesome country bubble have no problem coming up with the resources to feed their kids. Life out here in the country is wonderful that way. (Except maybe in some of the small Southern towns we've seen that are in economic depression.) At least in Madison, we have enough cereal so that no child needs to go hungry.

Cereal: It's Not Just for Dinner Anymore

From a health and nutrition standpoint, cereal is a common and not tragically unhealthy way to start the day. The typical bowl of cereal contains about 250 calories, the milk another 75, and a piece of fruit could get a young person out the door in a hurry at about 400 calories. This would be a pretty reasonable start for the day. Plus, the kids could make breakfast themselves while you are writing a blog post in your home office. In the grand scheme of things, cereal is a pleasant and thrifty way to feed a lot of adult people as well. A bowl of cereal, a cup of milk, and the cheapest food possible, a banana, can get someone on their way for under $1.00.

Crunching the Cereal Numbers

A 24-ounce box of Cheerios costs about $3.65 and nominally contains six 2/3 cup servings, except that no one ever eats only two-thirds of a cup. It is more accurate to say that a twenty-first-century kid will eat about 1-1/3 cups (or two servings) in a bowl. Even so, this still prices out to somewhere near $0.75 a bowl for name-brand cereal, not including the milk and strawberries. (Strawberries in season are about $2.00 per pound). At that rate, you're out the door waiting for the school bus for a little more than $1.00.

If you downgrade to generic cereal, the cost per bowl ends up on the order of $0.50, and if you go down to the level of oatmeal, this will costs you $0.18 per serving. Thrifty is good! Not to be too calculating about it, I suppose we are lucky in our little B&B bubble, in that we can afford non-industrially produced food and like it.

The Man Who Invented Breakfast

According to an article in *Forbes*, breakfast in America in 1850 consisted of "breads, pastries, pancakes, fritters, boiled chickens, cold cuts, and beef steaks." This almost sounds like the kind of good meal you could get at The Firefly, minus the beefsteaks. (Beef is expensive now.)

Dr. John H. Kellogg invented corn flakes in 1894 to promote bland food in the morning because he wanted to keep people away from sin. You will have to read the full article (contained in the Reference Links at the end of the book) to learn the exact type of sin that he wanted to stamp out. Kellogg, along with his brother, also ran what would now be called a B&B for healthy living. In addition to endorsing simple eating, the doctor promoted the health benefits of hydrotherapy. This involves bathing in water of various temperatures. If we could do that here at The Firefly, we might, but we would need multiple hot tubs. Since he was a better healer than a patent attorney, Kellogg faced many competitors who created knockoffs of his innovative cereal. One of them, C.W. Post, invented the Post Toasties.

NOTE: Battle Creek is still B&B friendly, and you can check into an ironic naturist B&B up there if you'd like the full sin-free experience.

Modern Sugary Cereal

Cereal, as we know it today, grew in popularity in the 1950s during the time when boomer children were growing up. The underlying reason for this trend was the plummeting price of sugar on the commodities market. By 1950, sugar basically became free. To illustrate this point, some of you might remember the café scene in *Back to the Future* when Marty McFly is transported back from 1985 to 1955. The scene is meant to illustrate what things were like in the mid-50s. Marty asks for a soft drink without any sugar, and the café owner gives him a cup of black coffee. (Does anyone besides me wonder why George McFly is eating cereal in the local high school hangout?)

The bottom line on this topic is that sugar was so plentiful and cheap, on an inflation-adjusted basis, that companies worked very hard to find a way to put it into as many consumable products as possible. A lot of work was done to market this stuff directly to kids or their 1960s moms, which was easy. As a result, today's typical breakfast cereal contains about 25% sugar.

The takeaway message is that people are wisely staying the hell away from packaged breakfast cereal. The cereal companies know this and are trying to sell cereal with less sugar in it. They are also trying hard to export cereal to places like India, where there are plenty of kids who like sugar just as much as American kids do.

Cereal Nostalgia

What does any of this talk about evil sugary cereal have to do with breakfast at The Firefly? Well, here is our philosophy in a nutshell. We want things to be as fun as possible for our guests. We are well aware that anybody under 70 likes to evoke pleasant memories of childhood (assuming they have any). Even though millennials are laying low on breakfast cereal, according to the latest studies, that same shunned product can also be used to evoke millennial nostalgia.

So, if you really want Fruit Loops or Lucky Charms when you are on vacation and staying at The Firefly, you should be able to get it. We can usually convince the Earth Goddess to keep some around just for fun. I think we can still get some of those little boxes that last forever and have just one serving. Breakfast for a big family or a small B&B means taking care of people by giving them what they like. We actually saw an example of this at the Bridge House in Atlanta, which is a fun B&B run by fun millennials.

Alternatives to Packaged Breakfast Cereal

Oatmeal with Nice Toppings

Who knew that oatmeal, the thriftiest and most austere breakfast food possible, could be made more pleasant with roughly the same toppings that we put on pancakes? This would be fresh fruit and nuts of one kind or another. Or syrup. (Sugar is sugar.)

Firefly Challenge: What happens when you put the syrup from brandied figs on oatmeal? More to come later on the topic of brandied figs.

Granola/Muesli

The Earth Goddess is tuned into the fact that Europeans and some Californians like the cereal known as muesli, which is a combination of dried fruit, nuts, and flakes of one kind or another. We do have sources for this locally, and I believe we occasionally stock some at The Firefly when we are expecting

Europeans. Breakfast for a big family or a small B&B means being culturally accommodating. Most Europeans like bacon. Californians have been known to go their own way and fend for themselves, and we gladly let them.

We found a homemade granola recipe at cookieandkate.com that we might try to make at some point. We'll video the results. After all, we can source most of the ingredients locally. Pecans grow around here. OK, maybe not oats so much, but we have plenty of eggs, and we like almond milk. The cup or two of maple syrup could present a challenge. Still, it might be fun to try the recipe since it has the same ingredients that we put in everything else.

Breakfast Bars

Breakfast bars are a suggested alternative to granola, and it is not completely unheard of for us to have a few of them around. These are popular with millennials even though (or maybe because) they have sugar.

This is ironic when you consider some so-called healthy breakfast bars are described with decadent names like double-layer caramel crunch. Are they advertised as sinful? What would the bland-food-loving John Kellogg think about such foods if he were still around? Apparently, breakfast for a big family or a small B&B means occasionally straying from the straight and narrow.

Yogurt

Yogurt belongs in this discussion because it is hard to tell when you have cereal with yogurt on it rather than yogurt with cereal in it. While we're on this topic, we should probably mention all the dairy products we have around our area, which include some nice cheeses as well as local milk. One of the milk by-products is yogurt—fermented, cultured milk.

Our permaculture heroes, the Rhodes family of Asheville, North Carolina, produce their own milk and milk by-products, including cultured cream and homemade yogurt. That is because they have their very own cow that they go out and milk every day. If you look at the Rhodes video listed in the Reference Links, you'll see that they are feeding their wholesome permaculture kids scrambled eggs from their own chickens, a little green stuff that looks like spinach, and yogurt with fruit beautifully served in an adorable country kitchen. (At The Firefly, we won't be getting a dairy cow of our own. We have all the livestock we can handle right now.)

Where We Stand on Cereal (Metaphorically)

At The Firefly, we're following the trend on breakfast cereal by cutting down on the sugar. That said, we still want to make your stay fun and happy, so we will go to some effort to come up with a nice, nostalgic, sugary bowl of Fruit Loops for you if you are on vacation from good nutrition.

We're just thankful for our abundance and well aware that we have enough space to create a wholesome little food empire here if we want to. In planning breakfast for our theoretical big family or small B&B, it might very well be a good economic strategy to feed them cereal 1950s-style. Well, it might not be so great for their health. In the process of feeding our guests what they want, we would teach them where to find the eggs. We've been getting five a day. (I still want to try the brandied fig juice on oatmeal, though.)

PS: If someone from the General Mills factory in Covington comes to stay with us, we will make sure to have plenty of cereal. "Big G, little o." Breakfast of Champions.

10 – Eggs or Weezy the Wonder Chicken

<u>Weezy</u>

We have a chicken named Weezy. She is old and came to The Firefly along with the first carload of our stuff. Because Weezy is lame and has a problem with her feet, this makes her different. In the chicken coop (as in life), if you are different, the mean girls pick on you. So, Weezy has a special little house of her own in the sun that keeps her safe from the hawks.

In the morning, Weezy comes to the back door to see if anyone is awake. If you're working in the backyard, she will sit on your foot until you pick her up because she likes to let people hold her.

In the winter, when it gets too cold for humans, Weezy is allowed to stay indoors. There is a little dog bed that is just the right size for her.

On the coldest day this winter, Weezy was standing in the breezeway. She had laid an egg right in the middle of the floor, where it could be easily found. This is unusual behavior since chickens typically try to hide their eggs. Was this a gesture of gratitude? Is it possible for a chicken to recognize and return love?

The rest of the chickens we have are loved in their way and give us their eggs as thanks for taking such good care of them. Does that make the eggs any better? We don't really know for sure. Holistic farmer, Joel Salatin, thinks that it is better for everybody if a chicken is allowed to be a chicken instead of an industrial egg-laying machine. For us, every egg is a Weezy egg—an egg laid by a creature who is expressing thanks. This is an experience you can't get anywhere but at The Firefly.

Our Emotional Attachment to Eggs

The subject of eggs deserves serious attention because breakfast in most of this country is all about eggs. Here at The Firefly, eggs are mostly associated with motherhood, comfort, and emotional attachment. Why? It's because the way we collect and how we use eggs for breakfast makes them an important part of our story. We've devoted a lot of time, energy, and effort to their production, consumption, and enjoyment. Therefore, our emotional attachment to eggs carries through to the guest experience at our B&B.

Of all the foods that people eat, eggs (well, chicken eggs) are the most mysteriously reassuring. This is because their shape, size, and texture physically evoke our caveman ancestors' emotional need for them. When prepared and eaten, they are considered comfort food. According to an article in *Psychology Today*, when people are about to be hit by a natural disaster, eggs are one of the three staples (four, if you count toilet paper) that they rush out to buy at the store. This desire to hoard eggs is not completely about nutrition. It has more to do with their ability to provide consolation in troubled times.

The History of the Egg

Eggs have been with us since the dawn of time. The earliest known eggs are thought to have been produced about 65 million years ago. We know this because perfectly preserved dinosaur eggs have been discovered that date from that era. This means that dinosaur fossil eggs have been around for 64 million years longer than humans have.

Paleo Poachers

When humans finally did arrive on the scene, our hunter-gatherer ancestors took advantage of the fact that all birds and most reptiles lay eggs. As long as these hunter-gatherers were prepared to deal with the potentially angry mother who laid them, eggs became a readily available food source.

There are a few different theories about why humans got the idea of domesticating egg-bearing fowl. One theory says it was because we had killed off all the mastodons about 8,000 years ago. With no more mastodons left to hunt, we needed to find an easy source of food. (Not that killing a mastodon is all that easy.)

Chickens in the Southeastern United States

According to Wikipedia, chickens did not become big business in America until after 1844, when the country began importing oriental poultry breeds on a large scale and crossed them with the domestic variety. Because eggs don't really need refrigeration, and the weather is good most of the time, poultry became a thriving industry in the Southeast. In fact, Gainesville, Georgia (up in the hills about two hours north of The Firefly) considers itself the Poultry Capital of the World.

In spite of what you might think, most of the chickens in this area don't lay eggs. Instead, they are destined to become menu items at Chick-fil-A and KFC. With the exception of the one on top of the town monument, you would be hard-pressed to find an actual chicken in Gainesville. That's because the biggest egg-producing states are not in the South anymore.

The discovery of Vitamin D in 1910 was an important development in that migration. Researchers found that if you fed your egg-laying chickens Vitamin D to make up for the lack of sunlight, you could keep them year-round somewhere north of Dixie. According to the US Egg Board, the number one state for egg production is a place where the sun doesn't shine very much, and people are smart enough not to kill their chickens. Here's a list of the top eight egg-producing states (numbered in thousands of egg-laying hens):

- Iowa – 53,044
- Ohio – 27,869
- Indiana – 26,4
- Pennsylvania – 24,244
- California – 16,261
- Texas – 14,786
- Michigan – 12,646
- Minnesota – 9,982

Egg Trivia: A football game known as the Egg Bowl is played each year between the rival college teams of Ole Miss and Mississippi State. The winning team gets a trophy called the Golden Egg.

Foghorn Leghorn

The big-mouthed southerner became a cliché thanks to the Fred Allen radio show in the 1930s. Foghorn Leghorn, the well-known Warner Brothers cartoon character, evolved from this stereotype (even though he was invented by a guy from Boston). Unlike Foghorn Leghorn, at The Firefly, we are, for the most part, tuned into the ecological balance among the four species (dogs, cats, chickens, chicken hawks). Therefore, the mysterious case of the disappearing attack rooster is a story that will remain untold for the present.

Industrial Chickens

We talked about industrial cereal a bit earlier. There is also such a thing as industrial chickens. The native jungle fowl, from which today's chicken is derived, usually lays 10 to 15 eggs per year. Today's factory chickens crank out an egg per day. This is because of selective breeding, targeted feed, and other engineering methods. These less-than-humane practices also include enclosing up to 100,000 birds in an industrial egg operation where they are force-fed and not allowed to move around.

Permaculture Poultry

The permaculture people believe that being earth-friendly is a good thing. Therefore, it must follow that a nice, friendly population of chickens will give you nice, friendly eggs. A lot of time and effort has been put into the study of this subject, and the "reverse pioneer" of organic egg production is Joel Salatin. He has managed to construct a little chicken and egg empire whereby he provides high-quality eggs to upscale restaurants around Washington, DC. He accomplished this by reverting to traditional and more natural methods of chicken control. Salatin even developed something called a "chicken tractor" that moves his poultry around his property in such a way as to graze, dig up, and fertilize the land.

Firefly Eggs Versus Regular Eggs

The next picture kind of says it all, or it would if it weren't black and white. You would be able to note the rich, golden color of the egg yolk on the left. It obviously came from a happy chicken. The correlation between happy chickens and quality eggs seems as if it should be an important enough topic to merit a book of its own. Maybe someday, there will be one.

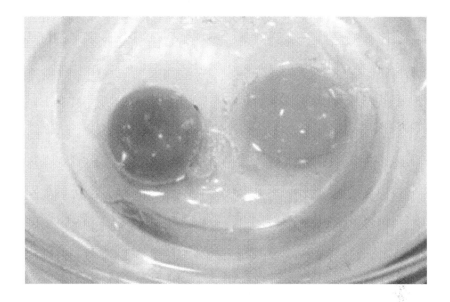

Egg Preparation and Consumption

We're going to approach the multi-faceted topic of egg preparation in increasing order of complexity.

Raw

Everybody remembers the scene from *Rocky* where Sylvester Stallone chugs down a pre-dawn cocktail of raw eggs. From our perspective, raw eggs are a hard pass. An argument could be made that Firefly eggs are less likely to have cooties than industrial eggs. Nevertheless, we don't advise testing that theory.

Rolled into a Campfire

Cooking an egg by rolling it into a hot campfire is tempting, but we still say no. Hot eggs are very hard to pick up without oven mitts. I should add that we are firepit-friendly at The Firefly. Maybe we'll try this option at some point if there is a guest demand for it.

Hard-Boiled and/or Poached

Hard boiling eggs might be a reasonable way to make them portable. Poached eggs are the same as hard-boiled, just without the shell. Neither method is exactly foolproof. Gourmet chef Alton Brown is an authority on this topic. Who knew that you shouldn't add a raw egg directly to water? That is unless you want to make egg drop soup (which is always an option).

The photo below shows a colorful layout of our breakfast table. The eggs are served along with tomato, avocado, a little ham, and smoked paprika. There's no rule that says hard-boiled eggs have to be ugly. Presentation is an important element of serving breakfast at The Firefly.

Egg Salad and/or Deviled Eggs

Food 52 has a nice recipe for breakfast egg salad. This is what you might get if you are around after we've boiled a lot of surplus eggs:

- 6 large eggs
- 2 tbsp full-fat mayonnaise
- 2 tbsp plain 2% Greek yogurt
- 2 tsp Dijon mustard
- 4 slices cooked bacon, crumbled
- 3 tbsp finely chopped red onion
- 1 tbsp finely chopped fresh chives
- 1/4 tsp salt
- 1/4 tsp freshly ground black pepper
- 4 pieces 100% whole-grain bread, toasted

This ingredient list has most of the items that we're talking about in this book, including the toast.

Diner-Style Eggs

With a little arm-twisting, the Earth Goddess could be convinced to prepare you some eggs diner-style. This traditional American method of preparing and serving eggs originated in roadside and city diners.

(An approximation of this diner atmosphere can be found at the local Waffle House.)

For the benefit of the Europeans (but not Californians), the lunch counter and American diner culture probably also deserves a book of its own. It, too, evokes a nostalgic response from certain people. Wikipedia devotes an entire article to the subject of diner lingo from a bygone era. Artists Edward Hopper (*Nighthawks* 1942) and Gottfried Helnwein (*Boulevard of Broken Dreams* 1984) both evoke the edgy loneliness of the diner experience in their famous paintings. At The Firefly, we try to avoid this kind of artistic gloom. That's because we are all about the delightful Earth Goddess breakfast experience. So, if you want "Adam and Eve on a Raft," it's not completely out of the question.

Omelets

For instructions on how to make a perfect omelet fast, thespruceeats.com offers some good tips. One of the best qualities of this dish is that omelets are forgiving. They can be prepared in a hurry with lots of filling fillers. Although Georgia is not known for its spinach, nor its mushrooms or broccoli, the Earth Goddess does maintain a supply of fresh vegetables.

Sidebar: The secret is out. Occasionally, the Earth Goddess needs to buy eggs because her supply dwindles. When this happens, she only sources eggs from "nicely-raised" chickens.

Frittatas and/or Baked Dishes

These kinds of dishes are super easy and can be made the night before. This is because, sometimes, the Earth Goddess needs her sleep and does not want to spring up and make Adam and Eve on a Raft. Emma Christensen wrote an article for kitchn.com that offers helpful advice on how to assemble a frittata with whatever you've got on hand. This photo shows The Firefly version of that concept. Most of the breakfasts that we do are keto-friendly but not necessarily organic.

Chain Hotel Eggs

We have to talk about the scary subject of mass-produced hard-boiled eggs now. The Sanovo Corporation invented a machine that can boil 20,000 eggs at a time and then peel them afterward.

Chain Hotel Scrambled Eggs

It stands to reason that if human ingenuity could invent a way to hard boil thousands of eggs at a time, the same could be done for scrambled eggs. Sure enough, there are now machines that can convert several pounds of raw egg into scrambled fluff in a matter of minutes. The question is, if you knew that's how your eggs were being prepared in the hotel kitchen, would you still want to eat them?

Frozen Hotel Omelets

I searched all over the internet to find out how frozen omelets are mass-produced but couldn't find any information. Evidently, "they" don't want you to know how this is done. However, "they" have taken out a US patent on the process. So, if you want to know how to make an "omelet type egg product," you can find out by checking the Reference Links at the back of the book, but do you really want to know?

If you aren't already a little frightened by what technology is doing to eggs, my research also turned up the fact that "they" have even invented an omelet-making robot. In case you're wondering, their version doesn't give you the same warm glow as Rosie, the robot maid who served eggs to the Jetsons. (Millennials may need to Google this reference.)

The Firefly Egg-sperience

For all the above reasons, we at The Firefly have an emotional attachment to eggs. The Earth Goddess goes out and collects them from the chicken coop in the morning. That's because she likes the chickens and has names for most of them. The chickens eat the bugs and grass that we have around the place. They are on the payroll. Therefore, they do not get sucked into the agri-business machine. The eggs are cooked by a human and served beautifully. Maybe there is a group of laughing, happy people ready to enjoy them. That's because it's part of an experience that you can't get just anywhere.

11 – The Art of Nonindustrial Bacon (and Sausage)

<u>Scene: Cooking Controversy</u>

Location: Family Kitchen
Time: Now

YOUR DAD: You can't eat that.
YOU: What?

YOUR DAD: That bacon. It's raw.
YOU: No, it isn't. It's fine if it's a little rubbery. I like it that way.

YOUR DAD: No, it isn't fine. You can still get bacteria. You can also get trichinosis.`
YOU: No, you can't. Do you know the last recorded case of trichinosis in this state?

YOUR DAD: No.
YOU: 1975

YOUR DAD: How do you know that bacon didn't come from some other state?
YOU: I guess you don't.

YOUR DAD: You're damn right you don't. They ship that stuff all over the world now. You don't know where the hell that stuff came from.
YOU: I'll take my chances. I got it over 145 degrees.

YOUR DAD: No, you didn't. You put it in the microwave and barely warmed it up. It's all I can do to even look at it.
YOU: *(Sigh and dump your breakfast into a cast-iron skillet while maintaining a sullen silence.)*

Introduction to Bacon (and Sausage)

We can't talk about the art of breakfast without talking about the art of bacon (and sausage). For some people, breakfast without bacon (and sausage) is like breakfast without bacon (and sausage).

The History of Bacon

For the enlightenment of the general public, historians have discovered the first appearance of bacon in 1500 BC in China, at which point the Chinese had begun curing pork bellies with salt. This advanced Asian civilization not only invented bacon but fireworks, opium, and they perfected the art of human reproduction long before the rest of the world. The word "bacon" originated in northern Europe and is one of the two words that sound the same in both French and German.

What Is Bacon?

It ought to be the case that everyone is in agreement about the fundamentals. We all know what bacon is. As it turns out, what bacon is depends slightly on what country you are from. In a general sense, bacon refers to cured pork or a pork by-product. Wikipedia has an authoritative article on the subject if you'd like to look it up.

In the United States (and also in parts of Madison, Georgia), bacon is the general term for cured strips of thinly sliced pork belly. It is more common to call this item "side bacon" in the rest of the world. We'll elaborate on the subject of pork bellies later on in this chapter. Before we get to that, let's spend a few minutes talking about sausage.

What Is Sausage?

Sausage is what you do with all the little ends and pieces left over from the rest of the pig. Some people make high-end craft sausage. Factories make low-end commodity sausage. The art of bacon (and sausage) is about beauty. We're not going to delve into the low-end segment of the business. You really don't want to see photos of that.

Fictional Versus Real Pigs

The pigs that everybody knows from film and literature are as follows:

- The five little piggies who went to market, stayed home, had roast beef, etc.
- The three little pigs, one of whom was bright enough to build his house out of bricks.
- Arnold Ziffel, the pig on *Green Acres* who could jump off diving boards and watch TV.
- Wilbur, who was Zuckerman's Famous Pig from the famous kids' book, *Charlotte's Web*.

The Zuckerman case is particularly interesting, and we will discuss it in a minute.

Real pigs, as found in nature, are smart, adaptable, and mean as hell. Domesticated pigs that have managed to spring themselves have overpopulated much of the country. Wild pigs can also get really big. Recently, a nine-foot, 1,100-pound feral hog was shot in Fayette County, which is about 66 miles away from The Firefly.

Industrial Pigs

Commercially raised pigs, like everything else that is industrial, are standardized. The size, shape, and body fat content of a lean hog are specified as commodities. Lean hog contracts are traded on the Chicago Mercantile Exchange. The part of the lean hog that is made into bacon is called the pork belly, and there is also a commodity specification for that.

A great deal of human energy has been devoted to economically producing the perfect pig. The people who do this sort of thing found out long ago that they needed to confine pigs, like industrial chickens, and feed them a standardized diet. The goal is to crowd pigs together to keep them from moving around so that they will fatten up quickly. The downside of this overcrowding is that industrial pig farmers also need to feed their livestock a steady dose of antibiotics to keep them from making each other sick.

The Unintended Cost

The unintended price that society pays for an endless supply of standardized pork is the stink. Where this practice has reached its full expression, namely North Carolina, managing huge pools of pig excrement has become a very serious environmental problem. It also poses a health hazard to the human residents living in the area who are forced to breathe an inescapable fog of methane (a greenhouse gas that is 25% more destructive than carbon dioxide). The art of bacon (and sausage) is not about getting rid of pig poop.

Pastured Pigs

The permaculture people believe in raising something called pastured pigs. Here is how the process works. You get a few pigs, buy a solar-powered electric fence, and keep a small, relatively happy, and non-stinking bunch of pigs. You move them around occasionally so that they don't root up the place (which they will do if left to their own devices). They don't need an abundance of antibiotics to keep them healthy.

The pigs hang out contentedly like this until they are big enough to make the ultimate sacrifice. When they get to the right size, they make a one-way trip into town. A few days later, you get your freezer full of pork chops (assuming you have a freezer). The butchering and meat processing is done by someone you know. This process is considered to be more respectful of the pig, who will be spared the horrors of a commercial slaughterhouse. Pastured pigs are thought to provide better, more meaty, firmer pork, and that goes double for the pork belly.

Where You Buy Your Bacon (and Sausage)

There is a school of thought that says the quality of your bacon (and sausage) is dictated by how it was treated when it was a pig. Therefore you, as a responsible consumer, should seek out pastured pork if possible. Our typical local source for pastured pork is the Farmview Market. This lovely place, which is about five miles from The Firefly, features pastured pork on a commercial scale. The Farmview sources its pork from Rock House Farm, which is 11 miles of curvy road away from The Firefly. So, if the Earth Goddess feels like she can afford bacon this week, the takeaway message is that it was born, fed, smoked, and sold within a 15-mile radius of The Firefly. Buy local.

Chain Hotel Bacon (and Sausage)

It's unpleasant but inevitable that we have to have a talk about how chain hotels source and prepare their breakfast meats. Chain hotel bacon (and sausage) comes in a big, stainless steel tub. Do you think the Chain Hotel Breakfast Goddess gets up at 4:00 AM and diligently stands in front of a frying pan to cook all those mass quantities of bacon (and sausage)? Of course, she doesn't. The truth of the matter is, somewhere in the vast pork supply chain, a high-speed bacon slicer will give you 600 perfect pieces of bacon per minute and feed them into a giant oven. A bagging robot at the end of the line will put them into a big container, which will then be sent to either the Hampton Inn or Arby's.

Do you know what it takes to keep a piece of equipment like that operating? An endless stream of perfectly uniform pork bellies. So, this is why chain hotel bacon (and sausage) tastes exactly like Arby's bacon (and sausage). It can best be described as bacon-flavored styrofoam.

The Local Art of Bacon (and Sausage) at The Firefly

Our breakfast meat usually comes from the Farmview Market. It is cut by a slicing machine that is run by the meat counter guy, whom we know by name. The Earth Goddess actually does get up and grill it on her little grill. The pig it came from grew up nearby too. Any leftovers will be recycled to the chicken empire, and any grease will be used to flavor something interesting later on. You will not get a bacon milkshake or any of a number of other bacon-infused products that are made with industrial bacon. What you will get is the delightful experience of good food, locally sourced.

Zuckerman's Famous Pig

The animated children's movie *Charlotte's Web* (1973) features a song in praise of Farmer Zuckerman's pig, Wilbur. This is the first recorded incident of a pig becoming famous enough to become a tourist attraction. Mr. Zuckerman makes more money from Wilbur's fame than he would by selling him as a few pounds of bacon and some pork chops. (The Zuckerman Farmstay is probably a B&B now.)

When you visit The Firefly for the Earth Goddess Experience, we will direct you to the local pastured pigs if you're longing to sing a chorus or two of "Zuckerman's Famous Pig." Please don't make us get one of our own. Friends don't let their friends try to raise a pig.

Cooking Controversy Redux

Celebrity chef Gordon Ramsay is a fan of fully cooked bacon. The internet consensus is about 80/20 that you should heat it up to at least 145F. However, a pretty solid percentage of consumers still adhere to the notion that bacon is cooked as it is cured and that you don't need to make it crispy. On that subject, I would refer you to the conversation that opened this chapter. The battle between chewy and crunchy rages on.

12 – The Only Right Way to Cook, Serve, and Eat Grits

Southern Comfort Food

Many readers will recall *My Cousin Vinny* (1992), in which a streetwise New Yorker tackles the legal system in small-town Alabama. A pivotal scene in the movie hinges on the question of how long it takes to properly cook a batch of grits. To southerners, this is a very serious topic and the source of regional pride because grits are a local staple that many people outside the South have never experienced. Grits are occasionally on the breakfast menu here at The Firefly and generate a lot of curiosity among visitors from Europe and California who haven't yet tuned into this regional comfort food.

The Origin of Grits

Grits are reconstituted boiled cornmeal. They are commonly served at breakfast in the same way as porridge (which nobody eats in America). Grits were originally given to the white man as a trick by the local Native Americans as advance punishment for conquering them and moving them out of their lands.

This food was first introduced to the original surveying party of the Roanoke Colony in 1584. The Roanoke Colony, of course, starved out, and the survivors completely vanished before

1590. Grits were later offered to the English settlers in Jamestown in 1607, but most of them survived the experience.

This low-cost, readily preserved food became a staple in the region between Texas and Washington, DC. The area has since become known as the grits belt. The epicenter is located in South Carolina, where the dish has become a particular favorite. Learning to properly cook, serve, and eat grits is a necessary element of surviving in the South. In 2002, grits became the official prepared food in the state of Georgia, however implausible that seems. Why does anybody need an "official prepared food?" In fact, Georgia is the only state that has one.

Grandma's Grits

Your preferred way of cooking, serving, and eating grits depends a lot on how your grandma regarded them. In an era when people aren't routinely in touch with Grandma, there is a gap in this generational exchange of culture. If your grandma was Italian, she might have been more familiar with polenta, which is basically the same thing as grits but ground from a different type of corn.

Grits are made from white hominy corn, while polenta comes from yellow corn. Clearly, Grandma had a lot of time on her hands because both grits and polenta take about 45 minutes to cook. According to at least one internet source, grits are more desirable than polenta because the texture is not as coarse. So, unless you are firmly committed to an ancient Italian family tradition, you might want to consider substituting grits for polenta in your next recipe.

Cheap Food for the Poor

According to National Public Radio, grits started out as a cheap food. The hardscrabble farmers in the South used them as a staple during the time when the region was economically underdeveloped. The *Journal of the American Revolution* refers to grits as slave food because ground corn was introduced to the slaves as a last resort. Later, grits were re-introduced to the slaveholders for exactly the same reason with some tasty embellishments. The accepted historical method to cook, serve, and eat grits is to boil them in water with a little salt until they reach the least undesirable texture.

Grits on TV and in the Movies

In the TV show *Alice* (1976-1985), reference is made to grits as something that is kissable. This was in the early, innocent days of television. If that show were aired today, they would just use the word "posterior" and call it good.

As mentioned earlier, *My Cousin Vinny* focuses heavily on the amount of time required to properly prepare grits. This information becomes a key piece of evidence in a murder trial. Have we told you that some of the scenes from the movie were filmed nearby? Check the Reference Links at the end of the book if you want to know the exact locations.

Grits as Animal Food

An article in rover.com says it is basically okay to feed your dog grits. It may be okay, but it isn't necessarily easy to do. Why a carnivore would eat grits in the first place is questionable. However, if cooked with enough cheese, butter, meat, and meat by-products, you might be able to convince a canine to eat them. Another article in sciencedirect.com states that feeding grits to your chickens instead of corn does not especially hurt them any more than feeding them regular corn would.

Waffle House Grits

Something needs to be said on the topic of Waffle House grits. (Our Waffle House road trip is still pending.) If you were to look at an online map of Waffle House locations in the United States, you would notice that the Waffle House map overlaps the grits belt almost precisely.

There is plenty to say about Waffle House as an idea rather than a place. The Waffle House method of cooking, serving, and eating grits can end up being many people's lone experience of the dish. There is some disagreement in this area, even among natives who frequent the Waffle House, as to whether their grits are worth ordering versus the hash browns.

Upscale Grits for Foodies

According to thespruceeats.com, as traditional southern dishes have migrated throughout the country, grits now commonly appear on the menu in upscale southern cooking. The main thing to remember about grits is that they are essentially tasteless. This quality means they can be combined with all sorts of different ingredients and served as a savory food. The most popular of these combinations are shrimp and grits, which originated in the South Carolina low country. If you add typical New Orleans spices to shrimp and grits, you end up with a nice high-end dish that can be enjoyed even by the snooty. (We are trying to cut down on the snooty factor at our place.)

While savory grits work well as an upscale dinner entrée, what if you're serving grits for breakfast? You'll have to come to grips with the central question of whether grits should be served sweet or savory. We'll have more to say on this subject later in the chapter.

Mistakes to Avoid

According to an article in the *Huffington Post*, the first big mistake to avoid in the preparation of grits is substituting the instant variety for the real thing. Once that pitfall has been avoided, the main grits mistakes are to under season them or try to reheat them in an oven using dry heat, which causes tasteless, lumpy grits. An alternate form of failure is to use too small a pan. Since cooking grits really means reconstituting them, they will swell up once water is added. If your pan is too small, you can expect your grits to drool out of the pot, potentially eating a hole in your floor.

Grits Disposal

Since grits are not considered hazardous waste, you can presumably dispose of uneaten grits in a regular landfill. There are also chickens in the area who would be happy to have them. If a chicken eats grits with egg in them, is the chicken being a cannibal? If the chicken then pops out an egg, which is then recycled into grits, is that not the purest form of recycling?

NOTE: Do not confuse feeding grits to the chickens with feeding grit to the chickens. Grit consists of little pieces of sand that are important for digestion since chickens don't have any teeth. Feeding them grits without grit is not recommended. (If you fed enough grits to a chicken, would its stomach swell up enough for the chicken to explode? There are so many questions.)

Grits for Breakfast at The Firefly

At The Firefly, you won't be surprised to learn that grits are a frequent breakfast option. Our B&B is near Atlanta in the heart of the grits belt, where people take this dish seriously. We may even feature a future seminar on the art of properly cooking, serving, and eating grits.

Most Europeans and Californians are interested in sampling the local food because they want to have a full experience of the region. The idea of an actual recipe here is a bit loose, but we'll do our best to explain the finer points of preparing grits as we go along. At The Firefly, the questions of instant versus regular and sweet versus savory have come down on the side of regular and savory.

How We Serve Grits (and Why Our Guests Love Them)

At The Firefly, grits are frequently featured for breakfast, but they can sometimes find their way to lunch too. I should mention that this dish isn't for everyone. That's because grits are an acquired taste. They serve as a background food that will take on the flavor of whatever you mix with them. By the way, all the photos in this chapter are of actual breakfasts at The Firefly. You can experience how they taste for yourself by booking a stay with us. We are absolutely convinced that the way we serve grits is the only proper way to prepare the dish.

The last time we served grits, it looked like the next photo, simple and comforting. The best cheese to use with grits is the kind you have on hand. Some online experts favor Pepper Jack. More typically, we like yellow cheddar to give the dish more color. Parmesan can be mixed in for a stronger flavor. If you have some smoked gouda available, the preferred method for eating it is on a cheese tray because this variety is too good to be used to flavor grits. Cheese and the other dairy products we use come from cared-for cows (and goats) and are available locally. Our favorite source is Amish.

Basic Cooking Instructions

- Grits (from a bag and not a box)
- Egg (at least one)
- Cream Cheese, four ounces per pot (more is better)
- Other ingredients: spinach, kale, sautéed sausage, onions, garlic, and anything fun that might go well with polenta.

Measure half a quart jar of dry grits and stir into a pot of boiling, salted water. Turn down the heat and allow to simmer, stirring often. Throw in egg, cream cheese, spinach, kale, or any other ingredients you may find around the kitchen. Stir gently while embellishing your grits. Once the grit mixture solidifies, you're just about done. This dish can be prepared far in advance if need be.

Just before you're ready to serve them, place the grits in a ramekin dish, garnish with a little cheese, and bake at 350 F, long enough for the cheese to melt and for the guests to sit down. This might take ten minutes or so. Add butter right before serving. This breakfast is served best in a big country kitchen, with laughter and a cut-up loaf of ciabatta bread and/or some selections of tea.

Sausage and Onions

Sautéed sausage and onions are also fine to add to your basic recipe. Smoked salmon is okay, but not shrimp. At our place, shrimp and grits would be considered dinner food.

Thickening Your Grits

You have lots of options here because there are thickeners for everything, and the neutral flavor of grits won't interfere with your thickener of choice. Flour is the go-to method for some people. This is because these people have sacks of flour on hand. Adding more cheese to the mixture can also be helpful. For most chefs, baking soda is the preferred thickener.

Grits with Fried Eggs

We make grits with fried eggs on occasion when the hens are in a giving mood, and we have surplus eggs. The presentation of this dish can make an eye-catching addition to your table. When the guest cuts into the egg, the yolk will run down into the grits and feel beautifully comforting.

Cheesy Baked Grits

When we bake grits, we like to serve them in little Pyrex casserole bowls, which can be placed in the oven. Add butter, cheddar cheese, and a little grated parmesan for flavor. Bake the whole dish for a few minutes at 375 F to create a little bit of browning around the edges.

GOES WELL WITH GRITS

Family-Style Grits and Sausage

When we serve grits and sausage, we often present it family style. A few pieces of sausage topping a bowl of grits is a pleasing addition at breakfast. We let the guests help themselves.

Local Grits

To the extent that it makes a difference, the preferred brand of grits around here comes from the Farmview Market. The market also gives basic instructions for cooking grits the right way. Aside from grits, as we mentioned earlier, Farmview has some good quality products, including local responsibly raised meat and meat by-products. We even know the butcher by name.

Grits and Protein

Around lunchtime, there is a way to use grits to make a feast if you add some extra protein. This goes double for leftovers. Take a look at the next photo. You can see how grits can make your protein supply look bigger and more elegant.

No less of an authority than Rachel Ray has a recipe for chicken thighs and grits that looks pretty similar to ours. Well, her dish is more beautifully photographed, but if you have a little leftover chicken, it can be turned into a wonderful lunch this way.

Grits, Chicken, and Vegetables

The main reason that grits were considered peasant food in this part of the country was that you could use them to stretch your meager supply of other ingredients and make a meal that would feed more hungry mouths. The dish in this picture features grits, chicken, and vegetables and illustrates this point perfectly.

Cajun or Creole-Style Grits

Cajun grits are fun to make. The dish in the next photo consists of beans, tomatoes, a little corn, and tomato sauce. It looks almost like you are going to start a batch of chili. A spoonful of grits in the bottom of a bowl with the feast on top is the usual serving method at The Firefly.

Cajun Shrimp and Grits

Even though we're trying to cut down on the snooty factor at The Firefly, we couldn't resist displaying this recipe. At the risk of appealing to upscale foodies, the next photo shows a nice concoction of shrimp, peppers and onions, all tomatoey, served over a bed of grits. In case there was any doubt left, grits aren't just for poor folks, and they definitely aren't just for breakfast anymore.

What to Serve Grits ON

When we talk about serving grits on something, we don't mean which foods you place underneath them. We're now going to ponder the fine art of presentation. Nobody talks about this subject too much, especially when considering a food as lowly as grits. However, it is important from a visual standpoint to serve your grits on something interesting. This is critical when you consider that grits, all by themselves, not only taste bland, but they look bland too.

At The Firefly, we use Fiestaware. The vivid colors and uniqueness of the pieces are always a favorite of our guests. It only seems fitting that we should use this brand of tableware since it is manufactured in Newell, West Virginia, which is at the northern tip of the grits belt where you can still find Waffle Houses.

13 – How to Make Toast Interestingly

Toast is so ubiquitous that we almost overlooked it in our discussion of core breakfast foods. Although it is basic to the meal, toast recipes can range from very simple to very complicated. This is because toast is so embedded in breakfast that it takes on the character of the person preparing it. If you are a simple person, your idea of toast is simple. If you are complicated, your idea of toast is complicated. At The Firefly, where you will find interesting people, we focus on ways to make toast interestingly.

What Is Toast?

I keep thinking that even in Europe and California, everybody knows what toast is. You take a piece of bread, put it into a toaster, wait for a minute or two until it pops up, and you are good, right? Wrong! We've come to find out that the origin of toast dates way back and, from the very start, toast was being used in unusual ways.

According to Wikipedia, the word "toast" first appeared in print in 1430 in a recipe for Oyle Soppys. The modern English spelling for that would be "Oil Soppies." The recipe ingredients sound as offputting as the name: stewed onions, stale beer, and a pint of oil. Adding a piece of toasted bread probably made those items slightly more palatable. Both bread and beer were dietary staples in Europe by the sixteenth century, and toast was often used to flavor drinks. Shakespeare refers to this practice in 1602 in *The Merry Wives of Windsor* when Falstaff says, "Go fetch me a quart of sack; put a toast in't."

The three variables in the preparation of toast are:

- The type of bread used
- The means of browning it
- The toppings and/or flavorings used to make toast more interesting.

Normal Toast

What we think of as normal toast is a part of the standard breakfast that first took hold in the United States in the early 1950s. For most kids growing up in that era, toast was made by your mom, who had time to stay home and prepare it. The bread brand of choice was Wonder, and the toaster of choice may have looked something like this next photo.

Although this version of toast is considered standard, the method of preparing it is relatively recent. It assumes that you have electricity (which was not the case in the rural South until the 1930s). It assumes you have access to Wonder Bread (which was only sold nationwide on a widespread basis after 1930). Also, it assumes that you have enough money to pay for all of this. For the majority of people in the Southeast, that was not the case until much later.

The more typical southern breakfast might have been corn-and-bean based. Things were different without electricity, the ability to store food, and the willingness of someone to get up and make breakfast. The references on the internet to primitive toast-making practices are very limited. A Ph.D. dissertation might be written on this subject.

Cultural References to Toast

The following pop culture references might make toast more interesting, if not interestingly. Movie buffs will recall the diner scene from *Five Easy Pieces* in which Jack Nicholson tries unsuccessfully to order plain toast in a restaurant that allows no substitutions to its menu. The Joker's urgent need to get toast no matter what the cost is truly scary. The second reference to toast comes from *The Blues Brothers*. Jake and Elwood Blues take a timeout on their mission from God to stop into a diner and order some dry white toast and four fried chickens. A third reference to the word appears in the original *Ghostbusters* film. In this case, Bill Murray utters the word "toast" to describe finishing someone off in a violent manner involving flames and incendiary devices.

Chain Hotel Toast

The Hampton Inn breakfast room has a conveyor toaster that can make 560 slices of toast per hour when turned up to its highest setting. I'm sure the factory model of this gizmo is in pristine condition, unlike the working model at the chain hotel where you will find toast crumbs and unidentifiable residue in and around it.

A truck driver and several giggling choir teens are standing next to you, waiting for their toast to roll down the conveyor. It never takes a mere ten seconds to make your toast because the unit needs to heat up first. The process actually takes more like two minutes unless the toaster has been continuously fed before you arrived. At The Firefly, you'll get the opposite of a conveyor-belt toast experience even though you might have to wait a few minutes for it.

The TED Talk on Toast

Some important concepts about making toast can be found in a TED Talk by Tom Wujec. Although he's really discussing systems model designs and process flow diagrams, he uses an exercise in which people have to describe making toast by drawing a picture of the process.

We can glean some useful information from this talk. First of all, you can tell whether someone is from North America or Europe by the way they make toast interestingly. The European method seems to consist of taking your bread, browning it in a frying pan with some tasty oily stuff, and putting a nice topping on it after it's browned. To most Americans, when the topping is raw egg, we call it "French Toast." (I guess we should have a conversation with a French person to figure out what they call it.) Secondly, the more people involved in the toast-making process, the more complicated the visual sketch of it becomes. This is not a surprise to anybody either. It's a miracle that anything gets done properly when there are too many cooks in the kitchen.

How We Make Toast More Interestingly at The Firefly

In the spirit of the aforementioned TED Talk, we had the Earth Goddess produce one of these process-flow diagrams, and she came up with what you see in the next photo. First of all, you can tell that toast at The Firefly, if it's on the menu, is made European style because the bread is browned in a buttered frying pan. Secondly, you can see that the most important element of making toast more interestingly depends on a selection of interesting toppings.

Bread Source

We should now give some attention to the essential topic of bread. The Earth Goddess likes to stick to keto varieties, but the guests sometimes want fresh French bread. Around here, when we need to source it, baguettes come from one of the high-end grocery stores in Greensboro.

NOTE: Bread is not keto, and we don't keep it around all the time. So, if you want a certain kind of toast, you'll have to negotiate for it ahead of time. You also won't find bagels at The Firefly. They're yummy but not keto. I think the coffee shop uptown carries them.

Butter

The Firefly butter of choice is imported all the way from an Amish source in Wisconsin. Locally, the brand can be bought from a shop in Athens, which is about 30 miles away. One of the miracles of the modern age is that some homesick northern guy with a beard can get butter like his mom used to make if he wants it. You will always find butter in The Firefly kitchen because it is also good in coffee.

Honey

We have a strong preference for local honey made by local bees. The trip to Farmview Market is shorter and better than importing honey from unknown bees who toil far away. You can also source local honey from a place uptown called the Madison Produce Company, which is generally preferred as a place to eat lunch rather than purchase honey.

Berry Toppings

The Earth Goddess has the scoop on locally produced berries. In the case of blackberries and blueberries, our source is very local because we have a variety of these seedlings newly planted and waiting to bear fruit.

Blackberry season in this part of the country is right around July Fourth. The wild variety is so plentiful as to be a nuisance that needs to be burned out periodically. However, for the people who care to do so, anyone can go around and pick wild blackberries for free.

The numerous methods of fruit preservation are generally known. If you have any unique ideas on the subject, why don't you tell us how you preserve berries? Better yet, come and stay for a few days and show us. Become part of our story.

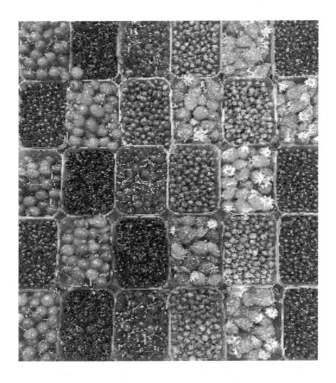

Peanut Butter

Georgia may be the home of the peanut, but the Earth Goddess typically just goes to the store and buys the crunchy variety of Skippy. We've learned through experience that this is the brand that just about everyone thinks of when you say the words "peanut butter."

When the Earth Goddess tried to serve craft peanut butter, no one liked it. Aside from that, the craft variety was too much trouble to keep stirred after the oil separated and rose to the top. In terms of other kinds of nut butter, our preference is for almond butter. It doesn't contain any added sugar and is keto-friendly.

Figs and Brandy

There is a story behind figs and brandy. Around Madison, legend has it that there is a crazy cat lady who lives by the tracks. When figs are in season, she sells or gives them away. In order to get them, you have to listen to her talk. This is potentially risky because it could take a long time for her to finish.

The proper method of fig preservation is to immerse them in brandy, which we keep for medicinal purposes. If you soak figs in brandy, the sugary fig juice will leach into the brandy and make an interesting syrup that can be spread onto some nice toast.

Miscellaneous Toppings

Avocado and tomato are among our current favorite toppings. Tomato season is almost here, and the avocados are especially good right now. We also have fresh rosemary and thyme growing around our property all the time.

Homemade Lemon Curd

There's a good recipe for lemon curd at tasteofhome.com. The Earth Goddess makes hers along these same lines when she has a couple of lemons. Hey, who knew that the recipe would call for eggs? We always know where to find those.

- 3 large eggs
- 1 cup sugar
- 1/2 cup lemon juice (about 2 lemons)
- 1/4 cup butter, cubed
- 1 tbsp grated lemon zest

Toast Points

So, what are we to conclude from this fascinating discussion about toast? You have learned that toast is who you are. You come to think about it the way you do because of a long story that went into its making. This holds true for toast at The Firefly too. The way we make toast more interestingly depends on each step involved, including the big kitchen itself. Every part of the process has a story. So maybe that is the essential point. The way to make toast more interestingly is to have an interesting story about it and everything that went into it. The reason you came to The Firefly in the first place was about the story. Be there in the square.

14 – House Rules or Always Knock First

Anticipation

For those readers who are planning to stay with us at The Firefly, skimming these pages has hopefully given you some sense of anticipation. We want you to look forward to a pleasant breakfast experience after you get here.

If you want something special on the menu, you'll have to reach out in advance. The Earth Goddess tends to make what she has on hand, and beautifully I might add, on at least your first day.

NOTE: Be sure to alert the Earth Goddess to any food allergies or other dietary restrictions you might have. We are very respectful of people's health.

Your Arrival

Of course, we recommend that you get here early enough so that you can look around the property in the evening. In the summer, a beautiful sunset from our front porch is especially pleasant. However, things being what they are with Atlanta traffic, a lot of our guests show up late.

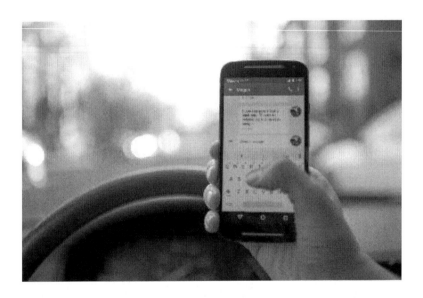

Traffic jams happen. Flights are delayed. People eat dinner first. Be sure to keep our contact information on hand. Send the Earth Goddess a text to let her know that you're okay. When you finally do arrive, you can park anywhere, but try not to block anybody else in.

Knocking on the Door

Keep in mind that The Firefly is a private home, and the Earth Goddess lives in the main house most of the time. The guest rooms each have electronic locks, and you will be given instructions on how to let yourself in. As you wander about the place, you may want to explore the main house. If you do, it's a good idea to knock first on whichever door you're approaching so that we know you're here. Texting is also good.

What Not to Do

We want to encourage our guests to feel at home when they're staying with us, but I suppose we should spend some time talking about what not to do. These rules apply to B&Bs in general. Do keep in mind that B&B owners are small businesspeople. They are quite often, as the Earth Goddess is, welcoming you into their home. They love to have you there and want to make sure that your stay is a pleasant one. However, as a guest in a private home, it's important to remember that you're expected to behave politely.

Mike from Mike's Road Trip surveyed over a hundred B&B owners to find out their top pet peeves regarding guest behavior. Here's a list of rules to keep in mind during your next stay at a B&B:

- Notify the owners in advance if you will be arriving late.
- Treat the property respectfully. It is someone's home.
- Be mindful of the house rules ahead of time (kid-free, non-smoking).
- Don't hoard amenities (snacks, wine, towels).
- Don't try to renegotiate the rates or terms of the booking after the fact.

What If You Don't Like What the Earth Goddess Is Serving?

You've just read through a series of chapters describing the usual breakfast fare at The Firefly. There's typically an egg/omelet dish of some kind coupled with fresh fruit and yogurt. There may also be toast made with some interesting bread. What if you don't like the kinds of food that the Earth Goddess is serving?

Please do communicate your needs upfront. You're going to a bed and breakfast that is staffed by someone who will tailor breakfast for you. We aren't like the chain hotels, where one size fits all in the food department, and everything is mediocre. We will do our best to be accommodating.

Skipping It

According to a study that was funded by the (ahem) King of Breakfast, about 31% of adults skip breakfast. If you add to that a late, high-calorie dinner, the combination is thought to correlate with heart disease. Skipping breakfast also tends to make you hungrier in the afternoon, which could lead to overeating.

A different statistic about breakfast can be found in a slightly more credible source than the above study. According to an article in the National Library of Medicine, 25% of people in this country skip breakfast. Our experience at The Firefly is that this number may be even higher. However, that's simply been our observation. It's not scientific, but it feels true anyway.

<u>Going About Your Day</u>

We're well aware that once you leave our place, whether temporarily or to hit the road, you have an entire day ahead of you. Whether you are working in the area or just passing through, we want to do what we can to make your visit memorable. An important part of a memorable experience is to appeal to all your senses in a lovely environment: touch, sight, smell, hearing, and especially taste. It's always our aim to delight our guests. We hope that you'll carry away good memories of The Firefly and that those memories will lead you back to us in the future.

Bonus Materials

Readers who want to delve deeper into the topics discussed in this book can find more resources online by visiting The Firefly website.

Once you access the URL below, you'll see links organized by chapter and topic. These will lead you to some interesting videos and articles that offer even more food for thought. Enjoy!

https://www.fireflymadison.com/references-and-links-goes-well-with-grits/

About the Author

Ellie Cowan is part of a team of busy innkeepers who manage a bed and breakfast located an hour away from Atlanta, Georgia. As the resident scribe of The Firefly at Madison, she chronicles its day-to-day activities. The property, guests, staff, animals, and food are all woven into her ongoing story of the bed and breakfast experience. Aside from writing, she teaches art classes and is a portrait painter in the Madison area.

After getting her bachelor's degree in literature from Wheaton College, she found a sturdy backpack, bought a one-way plane ticket, and spent four years wandering through Europe and Africa. While there, she developed a first-hand appreciation for the link between food and culture.

She is a fan of sustainable agriculture, natural medicine, buying and eating local food, and human-scale living. All of these preferences suit her small-town lifestyle. She loves chickens and animals but loves to travel most of all, especially to sunny, sandy destinations. Her motto is, "Live every day of your life."

With the help of online sources, she is currently researching her immigrant ancestors for a possible historical novel.

Books by Ellie Cowan

- Goes Well with Grits: The Southern B&B Breakfast Experience
- The Ultimate Southern Music Road Trip Guide
- Little Southern Towns: The Nickel Tour
- Big Southern Towns: The Dime Tour

Made in the USA
Columbia, SC
03 February 2022